THE FIRST SEX SYMBOL

To research this book the authors travelled 16,000 miles and interviewed the movie stars of Valentino's time—people like Carmel Meyers, Viola Dana and Gertrude Astor—and the Hollywood personalities associated with Valentino, including art director Harold Grieve.

Botham and Donnelly talked to friends of the star who until now have remained silent; and followed-up previously-ignored leads. Unwilling to accept the legends, they dug deeper—and came up with the sensational truth about his childhood, his sex life, and his mysterious death.

Journalists all over the world were commissioned to check allegations and rumours; and research for the picture section was exhaustive.

Ripping aside the mythology and mystique in which the publicity-built idol was enshrined, they present, in graphic detail, the true story of the real Rudolph Valentino: the story Rudy himself said was 'too wild and improbable' for his public to believe.

THE AUTHORS

Noel Botham was born in York in 1940 and educated at Dulwich College. He has been a crime reporter and a war correspondent, covering conflicts in the Middle East, Czechoslovakia and Algeria. He worked for the *Evening Star* and the *Daily Herald* before becoming chief reporter of the *Daily Sketch*. He is now a freelance series writer, working principally for the *News of the World*. He is married with four children, and lives in Surrey.

Peter Donnelly was born in Gateshead, Co. Durham, in 1941. He joined the Newcastle *Evening Chronicle* as a reporter, and later became a sub-editor with the *Daily Herald* and the *Daily Sketch*. He is now a senior sub-editor on the *Daily Mail*, with special responsibility for the paper's distinguished Diary. Donnelly first got interested in Valentino when, as part of a *Daily Mail* feature, he took a party of teenagers to see a Valentino film. 'They were knocked out by it,' he says. He has been digging into the truth about Valentino ever since.

Valentino

The Love God

NOEL BOTHAM
and
PETER DONNELLY

EVEREST BOOKS LIMITED
4 Valentine Place London SE1

Published in Great Britain by Everest Books Ltd, 1976

ISBN 0903925 494 (Casebound)
0903925 990 (Paperback)

Printed in Great Britain by
Richard Clay (The Chaucer Press), Ltd.,
Bungay, Suffolk

TO THE JOURNAHOLICS

If this were played upon a stage now
I could condemn it as an improbable fiction

William Shakespeare (1564–1616)

THE MAN ALWAYS knew he had an enthralling life-tale to tell. It was new, true and very often blue. It was Real Life Romance of rags to riches, fame with fortune, sex and sadness, poor little rich boy meets ten million girls-next-door. It was also far too good to be true, and Rudolph Valentino admitted as much shortly before he died.

'In my early studio days,' he said, 'I once tried to sell the story of my life as a scenario. It was rejected as being "too wild and improbable". To have one's life thus characterised, by a company which specialises in the most frantic serials, was rather disconcerting.

'Now, as I try to view my own historical record with detachment, I can see clearly what the scenario editor meant. The hero of my tale is not at all consistent, like a movie hero. In fact, I am not sure that he is the hero. At times he has all the appearances of the villain. Yet again, he seems to have good impulses, which a movie villain never has. Nor does my life run true to dramatic form. It should mount in a straight line to a climax. Instead it bounds like a kangaroo ...'

In that he was only too painfully precise: the life of Rudolph Valentino progressed in a series of spurts, sensational starts and stutters, right from the time he left the Italian hometown in which he wouldn't be seen dead and was caught up in and swept along by the ambition-powered currents of his New World in America. In and out of work, tumbling from the high-life to the low, plunging far below the breadline and surging back again,

7

he eventually shed the rags of the immigrant, amassed the riches of the successful, and promptly spent them. At the end of the rainbow he so diligently chased lay, cruelly, a crockful of misery, and below the mask of the gregarious, free-spending, apparently totally contented and fulfilled star was the world-weary face of a sad and often desperately lonely man, loved by millions in general and no-one in particular. The early, still-speechless cinema, that 'unnatural offspring of an unholy liaison contracted between the magic-lantern and the novelette', had made him as wealthy as a prince, as emotionally impoverished and pathetic as a pauper.

Only with his death came the spectacular finale that Valentino could not foresee as the triumphant climax to his wild and improbable story: elevated from mere, though adored, mortal, through celluloid sainthood to the throne of the God of Love, he became the figurehead of an idolatrous cult at whose shrine the unforgetful faithful gathered to worship, and the man himself all but disappeared in the clouds of legend. Even today a dazzling Hollywood halo still hides the human, and the pre-packed, publicity built persona is supported by the sort of adulatory biographies which owe more to the hysterical than the historical, to reverence rather than research.

What follows, then, is an attempt to find the facts shrouded by the fantasies and the fables, without the fans' worship or the film-buffs' theories misting the mirror. Obviously such an exercise could not be undertaken without the help of many people, especially those who knew Valentino well, and we have relied on them and their memories for much of the detail. Although they are not quoted directly in the narrative, we return to them towards the end of the story and want to thank them here, along with all the others whose help has been invaluable, for their time, their kindness and their patience in recalling the Valentino they knew.

Our thanks to Rita Maldarizzi and her sister Ada, Valentino's childhood friends in Castellaneta, to Gabriele Semeraro, the Christian Democrat mayor of the town for thirty-eight years, to the Commander of the Carabinieri national police office in Castellaneta, Marshal-Major Giovanni Cardenio, to municipal official Mario Gravini, and to our Rome-based colleague Ronald Singleton for his research on Valentino's early years.

To Viola Dana, Gertrude Astor, Carmel Meyers and Harold Grieve for their stories of his Hollywood days; Daniel Ullman, the son of his manager S. George Ullman; to Paramount Pictures, the Motion Picture Academy Library, the Los Angeles Library, the Screen Actors' Guild and to our journalist colleagues in America, including Kevin Thomas of the Los Angeles Times, Sandy Fawkes and Charles Higham. To Curtis Brown Ltd., the London literary agents, for permission to quote from *The Sheik* by E. M. Hull and from *Rudy, An Intimate Portrait* by Natacha Rambova; to the staff of Associated Newspapers' reference library for their uncomplaining assistance and time, to Nicholas Lloyd, Assistant Editor of the *News of the World*, to Margo Harding, whose typing of the manuscript was immaculate and immediate. And last, but never least, to the scores of journalists who covered the Valentino life-story as it happened and whose work and words, filed carefully away on yellowing newsprint, have been vital. To those enthusiastic professionals addicted to the journalists' trade, and to those who follow them, this book is dedicated.

NOEL BOTHAM
PETER DONNELLY
Fleet Street, May, 1976.

9

ONE

Yes, I am a fatal man, Madame Fribsbi.
To inspire hopeless passion is my destiny.
W. M. Thackeray (1811–63)

THE GREAT STAR, you could tell, was not only very, very angry. She was raging. She sat, furiously upright, on the elegant, richly-covered chaise-longue and tapped her right, beautifully-shod foot impatiently on the deep, dark carpet.

Nobody, but nobody, kept the great Nazimova waiting. And the Russian star was going to make sure that someone paid for this affront to her dignity and professional pride. She glared at the film crew who stood in a semi-circle around her on the set of *Camille*, amid a tangle of high-voltage cables, massive studio lights and hand-cranked cameras.

'Where,' she suddenly snapped, 'is that damn gigolo?'

Director Ray Smallwood glanced nervously at the huge studio clock. If that idiot did not turn up soon, the lady's notoriously evil temper was sure to explode in a snarling, spitting, spiteful solo. 'Who the hell,' he said, to nobody in particular, 'does he think he is? One picture makes it and he thinks he can keep us all waiting. Find him, Harry, will you?'

Harry Grieve, a young technical assistant who had worked on most of the set designs, nodded and strode off in the direction of Mr. Valentino's dressing-room. He knocked and listened. There was no reply. He knocked again, and opened the door. It was, he realised in an instant, not the best thing to have done. You wouldn't see it in the movies: they lay there on the day bed, with only her long black satin-lined cloak for a blanket.

A moan, of torment and pleasure, came from the lips of the beautiful, spoilt, headstrong and aloof Natacha Rambova, the girl they called 'The Icicle', the intimate friend and close colleague of the Russian screen-queen who sat waiting to start work just fifty feet away.

Her meticulously-manicured nails dug into the shoulders of Mr. Valentino, and her long white legs, those of a former ballerina, contrasted sharply with the olive skin of the man who would, in time, become the world's first and most enduring sex symbol, the Prince of Passion, the God of Love.

But this, as Harold Grieve's interruption indicated, was no time for love. Valentino twisted his head and nodded as Grieve quickly closed the door and went back to the set. Five minutes later Valentino appeared. He wore tails, a stiff-fronted dress shirt, patent black shoes and a satisfied smile. Behind him, patting her hair into place, came Natacha Rambova. She had won a significant victory.

Within hours, most people at the studio knew that the Italian's reputation as a woman-conqueror was not based entirely on rumour: he had not only thawed, but brought to the boil, the icicle Rambova. And yet, days later, there was even more sensational gossip being mouthed around.

Three members of the studio's art department, they said, had peered down from their office in a gallery overlooking the whole lot and seen the whole lot: some eighteen girls, aged between eighteen and middle-twenties, were lined up in an enclosed, rarely-used section of the studio. Casually, to the amazement of the three men looking down, they stripped until they were naked to the waist. And then Nazimova, accompanied by Natacha, moved slowly along the line, smiling, talking, running their hands over the girls' bodies. It was, they said, like some sort of weird beauty competition, and eventually, from the line-up, five girls were chosen and told to report to Nazimova's home that evening.

Shocked, and thrilled, the observers crept quietly from their vantage point to spread the word. Before long, it was common gossip, and the only man who refused to believe a word of it was Rudolph Valentino. Natacha, he swore, was the perfect woman, the girl who would one day be his wife.

In that he was right and wildly, tragically, wrong: the obstinate, fiercely independent, ambition-consumed Natacha would enslave, dominate and almost destroy him. People who knew them both would say that, because of her, he died of a broken heart.

And that she, the smooth and sophisticated step-daughter of a rich and successful American businessman, was a disastrous match for the simple immigrant boy from Castellaneta.

TWO

The childhood shows the man
As morning shows the day.
Be famous then . . .

John Milton (1608–74)

THE BOY, naked but for a pair of tattered shorts, shielded his eyes from the sun and stared down the rutted, dusty road that led West and to the distant, tree-lined hills.

Beyond them, he knew from the lessons of the parish priest, lay Rome, but that was far, far away, some 300 miles or more, and the farthest he had travelled was a mere twenty-three miles, to the coastal city of Taranto.

There, clinging tightly to his father's hand, he had marvelled at the tallness of the buildings, the multitude of horse-drawn carriages and noisy motor-vehicles which zig-zagged madly about the streets, their drivers hooting furiously on hand-worked horns, leaving clouds of smoke billowing in their wake.

That was where Rodolpho Guglielmi wanted to be. That was where life was exciting and fast and fascinating. And yet it seemed that his whole future, his entire life, must be tied irrevocably to this tiny, quiet town of Castellaneta, which lay, unchanging, unexciting, unmoved by time, in the instep of the boot of Italy.

He was born here, in the early morning of May 6, 1895, he was christened here in the local church, with that impressive army of names—Rodolpho Alfonzo Raffaelo Pierre Filibert Guglielmi di Valentina d'Antonguolla —and he would probably marry and have children and die here. It all seemed pre-determined, part of the plan that most people accepted with quiet complacency.

Certainly his father did. Rodolpho had heard him say several times that he had no ambition to leave the sleepy, uncomplicated community of little more than 6,000 souls, where he had found his bride, Beatrice—a beautiful, happy, always-laughing woman who loved to dance— and true contentment. And there was little reason for Giovanni Guglielmi to want to leave: the middle-aged veterinarian was, by reason of his profession, a man of some importance among the local farmers and peasants. His home, a square, flat-roofed house built of heavy white stone, and occupying a good position off the Via Roma, was one of the most impressive in the area. His wife, proud of her French origins, dressed more stylishly, by local standards, than the rest of her neighbours; and Rodolpho and his elder brother Alberto, and young sister Maria, had new clothes every year.

Yet despite his safe, secure and comfortable home-life, Rodolpho never seemed a happy or contented child. His beautiful face, which brought the kisses and hugs he detested from relatives and his mother's friends, was more often set in a fixed scowl than a smile, and his dark, attractive eyes were frequently lost in some private, personal daydream.

Now he stared down the narrow dirt road and longed to follow it to its end, to where excitement lay amid the tall buildings and the bustling streets. One day, he promised himself, he would go, he would leave Castellaneta for the wide world beyond that tantalising horizon.

It was a promise he would recall many times in the years ahead, but despite the aching, unquenchable desire to shake the dust of his home-town from his boots, it was noticed that Rodolpho Guglielmi made little effort to realise his ambitions by attaining any degree of academic success. When the local elementary school claimed him, only repeated beatings by his father, a stern disciplinarian, persuaded him into the classroom.

He much preferred to skip school and wander through the olive groves and orchards, taking fruit to keep away hunger, with his head in the clouds, imagining himself as a great adventurer, a sailor, a brave warrior. The scar on his right cheek, the result of an experiment with his father's razor at the age of five, was, he told friends, inflicted during a mighty duel (which he, of course, won). Maria often went with him on his voyages to adventure, listening to his fanciful tales and his plans for the future. Even the certain knowledge that a thrashing and a supperless evening loomed ahead could not spoil their enjoyment of the make-believe world he conjured in his mind.

But cruel reality was to invade that world. When Rodolpho was just eleven, his father died. He took the blow badly, weeping openly and unashamedly. Now everything would change. 'Now,' neighbours told him, 'you and your brother must look after your mother,' and he hoped, optimistically, that the change in his family's financial position might mean that his schooling would soon come to an end.

He hoped in vain: Giovanni Guglielmi had left his widow fairly well provided for, certainly with enough to ensure that his children's education would be completed, and before long Rodolpho—to his extreme delight, and the relief of mothers in Castellaneta with attractive teenage daughters—followed brother Alberto to study land-surveying at the Dante Alighieri College in Taranto.

16

He was boarded at the Manzoni Institute, a convent where both boys and girls were accommodated. And as the city replaced the town in his life, love replaced his earlier wild imaginative adventures, and the now darkly handsome youth graduated from childish hugs and kisses to sexual exploits of which he was to boast to friends.

Twice he was soundly beaten by angry fathers of girls with whom he had been found in less-than-delicate situations, which taught him only to be more careful in the venues he chose for his amorous activities. Attempts by his local priest to dissuade the young Casanova from his sinful ways, even the threat of certain eternal hellfire, were a total failure. And his friends Rita and Ada Maldarizzi, in whose home he spent more time than in his own, would never forget the day he brought back a ravishing young girl, a roving folk singer, and paraded impudently with her around the streets.

His mother pleaded and threatened and begged him to devote himself more seriously to his studies, even called in an uncle to apply extra persuasion with a thick leather belt. It was useless. Rodolpho refused to work, refused to study, and certainly refused to stop chasing girls, and his mother's hopes that the masters at his new school could instill some sense of responsibility into her son, and give his life some direction, were quickly dashed.

Their first reports were exact duplicates of all the things she had been told in Castellaneta: Rodolpho was either very lazy and inattentive, or very stupid, they said. He even referred to himself, with some pride, as a steady candidate for the dunce's cap. But when it came to stealing the heart of the attractive daughter of one of the school's domestic staff, he had no competition from his more studious classmates. He got to her room at night by climbing from the dormitory window, inching along a narrow ledge and stepping over her window sill—a regular excursion which explained why he occasionally nodded off during morning lessons.

He ignored repeated threats of expulsion, but it was only a question of time before that ultimate disgrace would be meted out, and it came about when his masters, angry at him once again, refused to let him leave the school to see the Italian King Vittorio Emmanuele, who was paying an official visit to the town—the first by a reigning monarch in living memory. Knowing his ingenuity when it came to defying authority, they stripped him to his underclothes and locked him in the dormitory. 'It's unfair,' Rodolpho protested. 'You cannot stop me seeing the king.'

His pleas were useless, but already he had a plan to get his own way. No-one was going to stop him cheering his sovereign—he who had strutted the streets of Castellaneta in a flour-sack cloak and a wooden sword, imagining himself a warrior knight. When everyone had left the school, he raised the window and followed the usual route to his girlfriend's room. He found a suit—obviously, by its size, belonging to a member of the staff—and pulled it on. The trousers dangled beyond his toes and the jacket covered his fingers. He smiled. It was better than running around the streets of Taranto in his underclothes. Not that he intended to run, or walk, anywhere. He would travel in style, on one of the school's horses. As he left the room, he noticed a large-brimmed hat and a sword. Just the things he needed to cut a dashing figure before the king. He grabbed them and headed towards the stables—to find all the horses gone. There remained only one small, mangy, donkey. It would have to do.

So, with the hat riding on his nose, and the huge

18

sword hitting the ground, he cried, 'For King and Country!' and urged the donkey onward to see his monarch.

Later, he boasted to his friends that no master could keep Rodolpho Guglielmi at school against his will. Their answer was not to keep him at all. Next day, with his escapade a bigger talking-point at the school than the king's visit, he was ordered home in disgrace to his mother. She wept in anger and despair. 'Have you no shame?' she asked him through her tears. 'If only your father was still alive...'

It was a scene to be repeated more than once during the next few years as the lusty young Italian's craving for travel and adventure grew more difficult to control. He made several half-hearted attempts to return to his studies, but each ended in further disgrace. Reluctant to study, obdurately opposed to any kind of work—especially that connected with agriculture—he spent his time lazing, dreaming, womanising and constantly pleading with his mother to give him enough money to travel to some place where he could try to make his fortune. To begin with, any place was acceptable, but gradually his preference hardened towards America where, if the streets were not exactly paved with gold, they were reputed to be littered with opportunities to make plenty of money.

One cynical relative laughed at his plans. 'But if every father of every girl you've pestered subscribed a handful of lira,' he suggested, 'there would be enough money to send you halfway around the world and set you up in business when you arrived.'

Rodolpho scowled. 'Laugh all you want to,' he said. 'But one day, when I've made my fortune, you will all be proud to be related to me.' Unceasingly, he argued with

19

his mother that the cost of sending him to America as an emigrant would be no more than what she had planned to spend on completing his education. Repeatedly, she refused to even consider the idea. 'Your place,' she told him again and again, 'is here with your family.'

But eventually his uncle, who had so often been called in to administer a beating to the boy, grudgingly gave him the support he needed to convince his mother. If Rodolpho was to continue in his idle, selfish ways, he said, and follow the vagabondish style of behaviour he had already begun, it would be better for the whole family if it manifested itself on the other side of the Atlantic. If there were Italians in America who would receive him and provide a roof over his head, and guidance, he would support his pleas to leave home.

Gradually, his mother relented. Sadly, she gave her wayward son her blessing for the step he had dreamed about and talked about for years. Rodolpho was overjoyed as, during the following weeks, letters were exchanged between his mother and a local family who had settled in New York.

The day his mother dreaded, and to which he looked forward with mounting excitement, came at last. His mother, fighting hard not to show her overwhelming sadness, kissed him goodbye for the last time. 'Don't worry, Mama,' he told her. 'I'll write to you often, and I will see you again as soon as I can. I promise.' Only when he had gone did she allow herself to cry.

Rodolpho's own sadness was eliminated by excitement as, on December 9, 1913, he set sail for a golden future aboard the Hamburg–America liner *Cleveland*.

His only achievement in Italy had been to leave it.

THREE

Poverty is no disgrace to a man
But it is confoundedly inconvenient.
                    Rev. Sydney Smith (1771–1845)

NO OTHER EXPERIENCE could quite compare with that of a young man arriving, for the first time, in America. Here, at last, was the much-vaunted land of freedom and opportunity, a huge, bustling, busy, thrusting place where every goal was attainable.

But to the immigrants it brought mixed emotions, ranging from blackest despair, through the still-fresh anguish of knowing that they may never again see the families they had so recently left, to a burning optimism and faith in the future. Now Rodolpho Guglielmi, at the age of eighteen, was among them, sharing their hopes, their fears, their private mental torment.

Later, years later, John F. Kennedy—the descendant of an Irish immigrant—who attained the highest possible goal, of the Presidency of the United States, would describe the Italians' lot in all its grim, graphic detail:

Most were peasants from the south. They came because of neither religious persecution nor political repression, but simply in search of a brighter future. Mostly farmers, their lack of financial resources kept them from reaching the rural areas of the United States.

Instead, they crowded into cities along the Eastern seaboard, often segregating themselves by province, even by village, in a density as high as 4,000 to the city block. Untrained in special skills, and unfamiliar with the language, they had to rely on unskilled labour jobs to earn a living.

They reached the new land exhausted by lack of rest, bad food, confinement and the strain of adjustment to new conditions. But they could not pause to recover their strength.

They had no reserves of food or money; they had to keep moving until they found work. This meant new strains, at a time when their capacity to cope with new problems had already been overburdened.

Soon young Guglielmi would learn the terrible truth of those words, but now, herded with other immigrants on to the lowest-class deck of the *Cleveland*, he inched his way through the crowd, straining to catch that first sight of the Statue of Liberty and of New York, with its towering skyscrapers pushing towards the clouds.

It was two days before Christmas, but there was little festive spirit among the immigrants, who had spent the past days crammed in the airless, windowless confines of steerage, their only escape from the odours and ceaseless din being this tiny portion of deck.

Even that privilege had not been without its price. For, as the ship angled steadily northwards across the Atlantic, the icy winter winds had brought their own kind of misery to the Italians, many of whom did not possess overcoats.

Rodolpho was one of these, but no amount of cold could keep him from the deck as the *Cleveland* nudged its way up to Ellis Island and, with straining tugs in attendance, crept to its docking place there. Chattering excitedly with friends he had made on the voyage, he was unable to tear his eyes from the majestic towers

22

that provided such an impressive portal to the land of promise.

Italian-speaking Customs officials eased his entry into America, and on the ferry to New York the company of other immigrants insulated him from the alien new world which now engulfed him.

But once alone, and unable to communicate with anyone around him, Rodolpho surrendered to terror, and for the first time realised the full enormity of the step he had so casually and impulsively taken. His friends and family were four thousand miles away in the sunshine of Castellaneta, and he was in this cold inhospitable ferry terminal with all his worldly possessions contained in the battered suitcase and canvas holdall at his feet. In his best dark suit, V-necked jumper and flat cap, there was little to distinguish him from the other young men jostling around him at the terminal exit.

They, at least, had purpose and knowledge. They belonged here. Rodolpho was overcome with a desperate feeling of loneliness and inadequacy and was sorely tempted to take the returning ferry and somehow beg passage back to Italy on the *Cleveland*—which, after a three-hour absence, now appeared to him as a warm, safe and friendly sanctuary compared to the busy, lonely streets of New York.

Eventually, cold and apprehensive, he plucked up courage to leave the ferry building—his last contact with his old life—and, with the address on West 49th Street given to him by his mother ready to push under the noses of passers-by, set off to find his new home and, hopefully, new friends.

In the dingy third-floor apartment, pathetically decorated with a few streamers and a couple of balloons in recognition of Christmas, Rodolpho was welcomed and cheered and inundated with questions by the four Italians who lived there. Two were from Castellaneta and wanted to know all the news about their families and friends. The others were brothers, from a different area in the south.

Warmed by their enthusiastic reception, and delighted to be once more the centre of attention, Rodolpho talked far into the night—at first in answer to their questions, and then plying them with questions of his own.

He wanted to know all about the girls. But, even more important, he wanted to know how to get a job: if all the wonders of New York he had just been told about were real, he would need money to enjoy them. Here there was no mother or family to turn to for cash, however urgently needed, and for the first time in his life, he seriously recognised the necessity to work.

The first problem to be overcome was that of language. His English was non-existent, and until he could communicate with an employer only the most menial jobs would be open to him. For six months he applied himself to the task while performing a string of unskilled jobs. Messenger, refuse collector, dishwasher and laundry assistant. He hated them all and was usually fired for insolence. Yet somehow he managed to accumulate the weekly fistful of dollars to pay his share of rent and food and provide a few litres of cheap imported wine.

He spent many hours walking the streets of Manhattan, touring the huge department stores, oblivious to other shoppers and a ready subject for the ever-vigilant store detectives. He marvelled at the range of goods on display and that there should be people rich enough to afford them.

He also learned that the girls, described in such

lascivious detail by his flatmates, were every bit as independent, available and sensual as they had told him. But their favours were strictly off limits to an Italian immigrant—particularly a penniless Italian immigrant—and the daughters of his countrymen were guarded even more jealously here than at home. The only way through those defences was a proposal of marriage, and no amount of frustration would wring that sacrifice from him.

By the early summer of 1914, Rodolpho's English was sufficiently well established for him to seek work away from the Italian quarter and, bidding farewell to his four friends, he left the West Side and moved into a stable garret adjoining the Long Island home of millionaire Cornelius Bliss.

He was employed there as an under-gardener, one of half a dozen on the estate, and in addition to his food and room, received the highest wage he had so far succeeded in earning—six dollars per week.

By this time his best suit was showing definite signs of wear and Rodolpho, spurred on by the example of his employer and his regular house guests, whose sartorial splendour quite dazzled him, determined to spend his first month's wages replenishing his wardrobe.

One of his greatest pleasures became observing his employer and the other splendidly-dressed gentlemen and women who came to the house. His job, he knew, was way beneath him, but he could make the most of this opportunity to study the rich at close quarters and try to adopt some of their mannerisms, tastes and tempting vices.

He became such a keen student of his betters' habits that he found himself spending more time spying on them than at his work—a fact that did not go unnoticed by the head gardener, who one day summoned Rodolpho to his office and summarily dismissed him.

Returning to Manhattan, he found his place in the West 49th Street apartment had been taken by a more recently-arrived immigrant and he was forced to rent himself a room of his own at $1.20 a week. Fortunately, by parading his experience on the Bliss estate before the parks superintendent, he managed to get a job almost immediately in Central Park.

Now, however, he had to provide his own meals and accommodation out of an almost identical wage, and the money set aside for new clothes gradually fell victim to his healthy young appetite. His main job in the park was picking insects off the rose leaves, an occupation which left plenty of time for thought and a continued observation of wealthy New Yorkers, who liked to stroll or ride through the park during the warm summer afternoons.

The one real thorn in Rodolpho's side was his immediate superior, a beefy Irishman who, as a member of one immigrant group in the city, delighted in having one of an even more contemptible group under his command. Each day brought its quota of jibes and sneers and orders to perform particularly menial and unpleasant chores over and above his regular work.

Finally Roldolpho could stand it no longer. After one especially difficult and trying exchange with his superior, he lost his temper and quit. For two weeks he tramped the streets looking for work. The occasional part-time job provided barely enough cash to buy food, and his rent went unpaid. After pawning what few items of value he possessed, Rodolpho surrendered his bags to the landlord and was thrown out of his lodgings. Other landlords reacted in similar fashion the moment they discovered he was broke, and now he was forced to wander the streets by night as well as by day—a homeless vagrant dependent on goodwill and the pickings from restaurant and hotel dustbins to provide his meals.

What sleep he had was snatched in shop doorways or on a bench in Central Park, where he cursed his hot temper and would have willingly begged for a chance to recover his old job. Without even a change of clothes, he was reduced to using discarded newspapers for linen. And his habit of sneaking into hotels to use their notepaper to write to his mother had to be discontinued because, with his disreputable appearance, not even the most unconscientious doorman could be expected to let him slip past unchallenged.

He lived with the constant fear of being picked up by police, discovered to be a destitute alien and either jailed or shipped back to Italy in disgrace. The only work for which he was considered fit was washing dishes and sweeping the floors of bars, neither of which paid enough to afford him a room.

On August 4, 1914, at the lowest point of his life, he trudged out on to the bridge across the East river. That Britain and Germany had that night placed themselves in a state of war did not concern him. The prospect of a million deaths in Europe was unimportant compared to the one death he was contemplating bringing about—his own.

In just eight months he had proved that he was one of life's failures. In this land of golden opportunity he had won for himself less than nothing. He had, as his uncle predicted, disgraced himself, his name, his family. His achievements were nil, his prospects non-existent.

In the centre of the darkened bridge he stopped and leaned on a guard-rail and stared into the black, swirling waters below. His mind raced, flooding with memories of home, his family, and his journey to this place which once held out so much promise. Despairing, he thought that to take his own life here would be the best course. It was the easy solution, and he had always taken the simplest way out of every difficult situation.

Looking again into the dark, cold blackness beneath him, he saw the reflected lights of New York, the city he had dreamed he would conquer and make the stepping stone to a rich and distinguished new life.

Suddenly he straightened his shoulders and lifted his eyes to the real city, back the way he had come. Angrily, he swore that a mere city would not beat him. He would not allow it to. 'I have the guts, and I can take anything America can throw at me,' he thought. 'What's more, I'll win.'

Thrusting his hands deep into his pockets, he turned and strode off back towards Manhattan, thinking, planning...

FOUR

They teach the morals of a whore,
and the manners of a dancing master.

Dr. Samuel Johnson (1709–84)

AT THE END of the first week of May 1915, America was
rocked by the news that one of the world's largest liners,
the Cunarder *Lusitania*, had been torpedoed in the
Atlantic and that many of their four hundred countrymen aboard had perished.

Would this, people asked, shake President Wilson
from his policy of strict neutrality and plunge America
into what was already being described as the bloodiest
war in history?

For Rodolpho Guglielmi, the significance of the *Lusitania* sinking, and the concern about whether his newly-
adopted country would enter the war in Europe, took
second place to his own personal problems and ambitions.

A few days earlier he had celebrated his twentieth
birthday in champagne—toasted by a group of attractive
young women who were all willing to hand fairly substantial gifts of money to the dark and handsome Italian
in return for his sexual services.

After his near-tragic experience on that bridge the
previous summer, Rodolpho had managed to find menial
work as a bus boy in one of the popular Italian restaurants between Fifth and Madison Avenues. And through

29

the other bus boys and waiters he had been introduced to the exciting new world of New York's dance halls and cabarets which, during the past five years, had become firm favourites with the sophisticated New York social set.

Single and married women alike used them as meeting-spots with lovers, or would-be lovers, knowing their afternoon or evening rendezvous would pass unnoticed under the cover of respectability these places had established. The only news from war-beleaguered Paris which interested these gay young things was the unveiling of a new fashion, which sent women's skirts soaring—to just below knee level.

Rodolpho, meeting the American girls for the first time in such an intimate setting, was fascinated by them. He found their fierce sense of independence, provocative talk and daring display of flesh stimulating and exciting. Compared with them, the women of Italy—even those he had fumblingly seduced in their fathers' barns—were modestly retiring creatures who uncomplainingly accepted their role as second-class citizens.

In the cabarets of New York the girls picked the men they wanted, and on their terms. A girl could pay a man to dance with her, to sit with her and, if he took her fancy, to make love to her in a room which she often arranged and paid for.

The name given to these male dancers was 'gigolo'. Used and enjoyed by the American female, to the American male they were a popular target for abuse, lavatory humour and even physical assault. But to the sexually deprived Rodolpho the role of gigolo presented itself as one of the most desirable and enviable professions he had yet encountered. The only problem was that, at the moment, he could not dance.

That did not prevent him going to the dance halls as frequently as his job allowed, and he was soon able to describe himself as 'one of the best wallflowers in the city of New York. I support more ballroom walls than any other man I've heard of,' he said.

Finally, one of the older waiters came to his rescue and taught him the basic steps of the waltz and the tango, which had been imported from South America via Europe and was currently the rage of America.

With that and his striking foreign appearance, deep, heavily-accented voice and almost hypnotic eyes—which when viewed from just a few inches while dancing awoke in most women an unsuppressible sexual turmoil—he was set for success.

Within a few weeks he was sufficiently proficient and confident enough to seek full-time work as a dance partner. The cabaret owner advanced him the price of evening clothes and some free advice: 'With your looks and manners, you're going to spend a lot more time in bed with your partners than on the dance floor. Make sure you do it in your time and not mine.'

What Rodolpho soon began to term his 'love break' came between the end of the afternoon, or tea dance, session, and the late evening festivities—a period to give the dancers a chance to relax and change from the afternoon lounge suits to formal evening wear.

Rodolpho found little opportunity for relaxation. He was an instant success with the unescorted female customers, both young and middle-aged, and the subject of frequent squabbles between sex-hungry society women who would dash to claim him when he made his entrance on the floor.

Within a few weeks he was earning a regular six dollars a day—equivalent to his full week's money as a

31

gardener—and by his twentieth birthday was occupying a smart two-roomed apartment of his own on East 61st Street and boasting a growing wardrobe of fashionable suits and jackets.

With success came discrimination. As the cabaret owner had predicted, most of his admirers wanted him in their beds moving in time to their own particular brand of music. But Rodolpho, his eighteen months of enforced celibacy well and truly dissipated, became far more selective in his choice of companions.

Money alone was no longer the key which released the young Latin's passion. Beauty and breeding were now the main factors involved.

Beauty there was in plenty, but for genuine breeding and really high society, he had to look to one of the more famous cabarets—Maxim's, Bustanoby's or Delmonico's. For this reason, he began to concentrate less on the sexual side of a gigolo's life and more on the dancing.

Eventually he was satisfied that his dancing had reached the professional standard required at Maxim's. His interpretation of the tango especially won him applause in the dance hall where he worked, and for several weeks the owner had paid extra for a demonstration of the dance, even providing a professional partner to perform with him.

At the same time, Guglielmi had worked on his other attributes. Hours spent before a mirror had enabled him to perfect the smouldering-eyed look which seemed to mesmerise his customers. He had the waist and hips of his evening suit trousers taken in an extra inch, and brought his deep bow and kissing of hands to a well-choreographed excellence.

He shaved off the moustache he had grown during the previous year and took to using generous applications of brilliantine on his thick, dark hair so he could keep it slickly combed to his scalp.

His looks and manners, he knew, might seem effeminate to other men, but for Rodolpho Guglielmi they were all valuable tools of his trade. The director in charge of the exhibition dances and gigolos at Maxim's agreed, and hired the Italian on the spot.

The move to Maxim's successfully helped Rodolpho over another personal hurdle—a decision with which he had been struggling for some weeks. The ladies at the cabaret complained that they found it extremely difficult to remember his other name—Guglielmi. Rodolpho, they told him, required something far more romantic, and for the first time in his life he was thankful for the many names of his baptism. Somewhere among them ought to be one that sounded romantic to American ears. According to family tradition, the name di Valentina was a Papal title bestowed on one of their ancestors for some long-forgotten deed of valour on behalf of the Holy Father. With very little embellishment, it was a story which could provide a highly-romantic piece of nonsense to trot out if he were ever questioned about his name. If the ladies at the dance hall gave their approval, then di Valentina it would be.

As he whispered words of love into the receptive ears of his trembling partners, Rodolpho tried out his new name, and as the syllables rolled off his tongue, they smiled even more delightedly and hugged him closer. He had chosen well.

On his first night at Maxim's, as he took the floor with his new partner to give an exhibition of ballroom dancing, he heard the name publicly aired for the first time by the master of ceremonies: Mister Rodolpho di Valentina. Appearance, name and dancing skill all made an

33

immediate impact, and half an hour later, when he became free to dance with the customers, he found himself at the centre of a group of elegant and bejewelled women of various ages who wanted to be the first partner of this arrogant and deliciously handsome Continental who danced the tango as though it had been invented for him.

Almost overnight, Rodolpho became the most popular dancer at Maxim's—which meant the most popular on the New York cabaret circuit. Like a Broadway star, he began to receive bouquets, toilet waters, silk handkerchiefs and other small gifts from his admirers and, increasingly, he was invited by performers in other entertainment spheres to their homes and parties.

In his letters to Castellaneta, Rodolpho no longer had reason to exaggerate his position in America. He was now earning seventy dollars per week—good pay even by American standards—and in comparison to his old neighbours in Italy, a vast figure. But now that he had the means, he never thought to send money back to his mother, who had financed his passage to this new world out of her limited widow's bequest.

So popular had he become that, though some of the men still sneeringly referred to him as a lounge lizard or gigolo, and Maxim's expected him to dance occasionally with a favoured lady customer, he was no longer open to offers of payment for physical acts of love.

If he did deign to dance with one of his admirers, it was universally understood that the minimum tip he would be prepared to accept was five dollars. Highly-sensitive to slights of any kind, temperamental and disdainful of his competitors, di Valentina was rapidly becoming the prima donna of the Manhattan cabaret set. But his popularity was immense, and it was only a matter of time before he, too, would find someone to admire

34

passionately.

That time came one evening as he chatted to two Ziegfeld Follies girls who were doing the town with a pair of wealthy stage-door Johnnies. Rodolpho was beckoned to one side by the head waiter, who earned substantial tips from rich clients wanting to dance or even sit for a few minutes with di Valentina.

Nodding towards one of the ringside tables where three women sat, he whispered: 'The dark-haired beauty on the right is hot for you. And she has plenty. That's Jack de Saulles' wife.'

Rodolpho glanced across the dance floor and stiffened. The famous enigmatic smile, so carefully perfected in front of the mirror, slipped from his face. He was looking at one of the most beautiful women he had ever encountered, with large liquid eyes, full ripe lips and gleaming black hair which shimmered as she laughed at a comment from one of her companions. A glittering diamond pendant hung in the honey-tanned V where a daringly-cut gown exposed more than a promise of the sensational frontage that seemed a direct challenge to every red-blooded male in the cabaret.

Unconsciously, Rodolpho reached up a hand to pat his patent leather hair into place. For once, the head waiter noted smugly, the handsome dancer had been thrown off balance.

'Do you like it?' he asked.

'Sensational,' said di Valentina. 'You may present me to the lady.' And, almost as an afterthought, he added: 'Tell the orchestra that I will dance the tango.'

It was to prove a fateful, fatal choice of number.

FIVE

What passion cannot music raise and quell!
John Dryden (1631–1700)

RODOLPHO bowed low. The woman smiled and nodded. The music began as they walked together on to the floor. So this, he thought, as he took her into his arms for the first of many times, was Bianca de Saulles, the woman he had heard so much about.

The beautiful South American heiress, he knew, had been married four years ago to Jack de Saulles, a well-known and wealthy New York social figure.

The onetime Yale quarterback and football team captain had met the former Senorita Errazuriz during a business visit to Chile, where she lived with her equally beautiful and fabulously wealthy mother, and the girl-crazy American chased her to Spain and then to France and eventually married her in Paris.

But within a year of their return to New York, the ex-footballer tired of his exotic young wife. He was a man who craved variety in his sexual relationships and found it among the chorus girls and bit players of New York's theatreland.

Bianca, young and vibrant, her passions aroused and her Latin temper fuelled by her husband's constant infidelity, decided to pay him back in kind. She had the money and the friends to speed her plans to fruition, and together they had brought her to Maxim's and into the arms of Rodolpho di Valentina.

Other couples gradually melted to the edges of the dance floor as the striking pair, seemingly oblivious to their surroundings, swayed, glided and turned to the passionate and romantic rhythm of the tango. So immediate was their understanding of each other that the Italian and the South American might have practised this dance together since childhood.

'You have stolen my heart completely,' whispered Rodolpho as his lips brushed her ear.

'You are everything I have been searching for,' answered Bianca, her whole body, from demanding breasts to trembling knees, held tightly to his.

As the dance ended, and the applause and cheers of the Maxim's clientele swelled about them, Rodolpho and Bianca arranged their assignation for the following day.

When he returned to the employees' table near the orchestra after escorting the dark-haired temptress back to her place, one of the other gigolos slapped him on the shoulder: 'I envy you getting a grip on that little number,' he smirked.

Rodolpho froze and glared at the other dancer. 'How dare you even comment on her,' he snarled. 'She is the woman to whom I have given my love.'

In his apartment the following day, and on numerous other days during the following year, Rodolpho and Bianca gave full release to the passions they had needed all their willpower to restrain on the dance floor. During these illicit meetings she told him of her loneliness in the great mansion where she spent so much of her time with only the servants as company, and of the vileness of her husband who made not the slightest effort to conceal his adulterous affairs.

Rodolpho wept for her, sympathised with her and

promised her his everlasting love. He said later of his feelings for her: 'I was dazzled by the radiance of her beauty. She was the princess I'd rescued so often in my boyish imagination. When we danced, she was very happy. But afterwards her tears told me of the weight of her heart—loneliness for her homeland and bitter sorrow at the break-up of her marriage.'

She loved him in return, but in the end it was his relationship with her which was to trigger his hasty departure from New York—a move which would eventually bring him international fame and immortalise him as the world's greatest lover.

Throughout the year of his affair with Bianca, Rodolpho remained completely faithful to her, creating certain difficulties at Maxim's, where he was plagued nightly by amorous females wishing to put him through his paces.

And it was Bianca who would get him away from all that by first suggesting that he consider showbusiness as a career. 'You're as good as any professional dancer I've seen,' she told him. 'Why not team up with another professional and give exhibitions full time?'

It seemed like good advice to Di Valentina. Complaints of male prostitution had led to some of the gigolos being questioned by the New York Vice Squad and leading society figures were beginning to avoid the cabarets for fear of finding themselves at the centre of a scandal.

By chance one of his admirers invited him to a party which was also attended by Bonnie Glass, an attractive and shapely performer from Massachusetts who had eloped with the son of a well-heeled local family and divorced him three years later. She was then in the process of dissolving her dancing act with Clifton Webb and needed a new partner.

After dancing only a few steps with the lean-hipped

Italian, Bonnie made him a proposition. She was prepared to pay him fifty dollars a week to be her new partner. It was well under half what he was earning at Maxim's, but di Valentina barely hesitated. It was probably the best opportunity he would get to 'turn legitimate' and become a recognised professional performer, and it would get him away from the clutching fingers of the barracuda-like sex-seekers in the cabaret.

He took her hand and kissed it. 'I will be delighted to accept your offer,' he told her. But his delight soon turned to disillusion and resentment when the couple opened at the Winter Garden and Rodolpho discovered that Bonnie, an established box office draw, was paid far more than himself. After the Winter Garden, they appeared in a string of other New York theatres and were a smash hit with the public.

Egged on by Bianca, who felt he was being exploited, Rodolpho repeatedly pressed his dancing partner for a more equal share of their earnings. But Bonnie was immovable. If Rodolpho was dissatisfied, she said, he could pull out of the partnership any time that suited him. She could easily find herself another good-looking hoofer. Rodolpho believed she was bluffing, but dare not put it to the test.

With typical contrariness, however, Bonnie took over the old Boulevard Café and reopened it as the Montmartre—doubling di Valentina's salary to one hundred dollars a week.

An all-expenses paid tour of the Eastern seaboard cities followed, culminating in a memorable performance before President Wilson in Washington, which Rodolpho graphically described in a letter to his mother. If he had not yet become President, he'd at least danced before one.

39

Italy was now at war with Germany, and the Guglielmi family was suffering both financially and from a lack of food, in common with most of their countrymen in southern Italy. But the conflict across the Atlantic was not Rodolpho's concern and, if asked, he explained he preferred to stick to the policies of his adopted country. Like himself, America was non-aggressive and strictly neutral. Italy must have been badly advised to enter the war on the side of the Allies, he said.

Platitudes for his new country, gentle criticism of his birthplace and a smooth relationship with his partner. Rodolpho di Valentina was basking in his spotlit reputation and enjoying the rewards it brought him. He wanted nothing he did or said to upset this long sought and deeply-appreciated comfortable life style.

His ambitions were truly satisfied, and had circumstances not so rudely dislodged him from his contented niche, it is doubtful if he would have made further efforts of his own to achieve greatness.

But the first of a series of shocks and setbacks was only days away as winter turned into the spring of 1916. After their triumph on the Keith vaudeville circuit, Bonnie Glass decided to start yet another cabaret in New York. The Chez Fisher opened on West Fifty-Fifth Street to long queues and was a roaring success from the beginning. But, unbeknown to her dancing partner, Bonnie was planning a partnership of a very different kind.

The news of her engagement to a multi-millionaire staggered Rodolpho. The realisation that she was to quit dancing and close the cabaret floored him. Suddenly, when it had seemed that nothing but success lay ahead of him—even prompting him to consider marriage to Bianca—he was thrown back among the regiments of the unemployed.

There was, however, a pleasant surprise awaiting him. Although Bonnie had always been the star of their act, during the year they had danced together Rodolpho had established his own, not large, but faithful following among theatregoers. A showbusiness agent had little trouble booking him into a tour with a string of unknown dance partners at 150 dollars per week—far more than Bonnie (soon to be Mrs. Ben Ali Haggin) had paid.

Good fortune continued to smile upon him. When that tour ended he was invited to audition as partner to Joan Sawyer, one of the country's most talented and highly-paid exhibition dancers.

The audition went well and Miss Sawyer expressed herself well satisfied with his abilities as a dancer, but she was scarcely able to conceal her contempt for him as a man. Imperiously she stated her terms, which she quite clearly considered ridiculously generous to this Italian immigrant—and on his acceptance, dismissed him from her presence.

Smarting under her calculated rudeness, but not so rash as to throw away the chance of linking his name with that of such a famous personality, Rodolpho turned for consolation to Bianca de Saulles. Their affair, which they still conducted in great secrecy, burned with all the uninhibited passion of its beginning, more than a year before.

The ivory-skinned wife of the Wall Street lecher still held a great attraction for the young Italian. She gave him her body willingly and as often as possible in a rite of love which never failed to carry him to indescribable heights of ecstacy. Afterwards, as they lay, satiated and drowsy in each others' arms, she told him of her husband's bullying, drunken treatment of her and his boasting of his sexual exploits with other women. And

41

Rodolpho complained of his latest dance partner's superior pose and scornful comments backstage.

On one such occasion Rodolpho suggested the possible way in which both their partnership problems could be resolved. If they could prove adultery between the pair— the only grounds for divorce in the State—Bianca could gain her freedom and she and Rodolpho could marry.

In public Jack de Saulles still needed to maintain the pretence that his marriage was working, and reluctantly, with boorish lack of grace, occasionally escorted Bianca to one of New York's social events. It was arranged between the lovers that Rodolpho would present Joan Sawyer to de Saulles after their performance at one of the city's nightspots if Bianca could persuade him there. The beefy estate agent's determination to physically possess every beautiful woman to whom he was introduced—and many to whom he was not—would do the rest.

By innocently mentioning that two of New York's most famous socialites were in the audience, and that he knew Mrs. de Saulles slightly, Rodolpho ensnared his social-climbing partner and she was more than willing to be presented.

The satyr in de Saulles must have been working over-time that night. Rodolpho could see him mentally licking his lips as he ogled the beautiful brunette dancer, and was hardly surprised when his lover's husband reappeared later at the club—this time alone—and insisted on buying champagne for Miss Sawyer.

Shortly afterwards, papers were served on de Saulles for divorce, naming Joan Sawyer as co-respondent. Within minutes the dancer had also been informed, and when the name Rodolpho Guglielmi was revealed as one of the principal witnesses, she screamed for her partner. White-faced with fury, eyes blazing and spitting her words like daggers, she informed him that he could from that instant consider himself a solo act once more.

In the divorce hearing, which began towards the end of July 1916, Rodolpho told how he had accompanied Joan Sawyer to de Saulles' 'bachelor' apartment and how he had seen the couple together in an hotel. Evidence from Joan Sawyer's cook and the estate agent's valet clinched the case.

On September 15, Bianca heard that her divorce had been granted. But Rodolpho was unable to be with her to celebrate. He was in the office of the District Attorney being questioned in connection with an investigation into graft. Acting on information suspected to have come from sources close to Jack de Saulles, detectives had raided a flat in New York two weeks earlier.

The information claimed that a bogus nobleman, Rodolpho Guglielmi, was using the flat as a base for blackmail operations against rich New Yorkers who might find themselves in embarrassing divorce scandals. Rodolpho claimed that he was being framed and eventually, after questioning from the District Attorney's assistants, the charges were quietly dropped.

But the incident had soured Rodolpho against the name de Saulles and, fearing reprisals from Bianca's former husband if he openly took up his previous relationship with her, he opted for another dance tour with a group of comparative unknowns outside New York and bid her a brief, far-from-fond, farewell.

This tour was followed by a series of undistinguished bookings at theatres in New York and an occasional exhibition at Maxim's. The number of theatres still able to book professional dancers was dwindling, and Rodolpho was now having to consider poorly-paid engagements to dance the prologue before the full-length feature movies now being turned out in Hollywood—a tiny suburb of Los Angeles three thousand miles from New York.

'You'd be better off dancing in pictures than in front of them,' one theatre manager advised him. 'There's a heck of a lot of money being made by young fellows like you out there. Why not give it a try?'

The advice was good. But Rodolpho was still undecided. Dancing exhibitions weren't entirely played out and it would be a big risk trying to break into an industry of which he had absolutely no knowledge.

Then, on August 3, 1917, something happened that made up Rodolpho's mind for him: Bianca de Saulles shot and killed her ex-husband in an argument over custody of their child. She was immediately arrested and sent for trial in November.

Fearing his previous rather sordid connections with his former lover could be dragged into the case, and far from easy over his position with the police—who could still deport him on a technicality if they chose to—Rodolpho decided to head West.

It was a great comedown for the 'top of the bill' dancer, but he accepted a job as chorus boy in a light-weight musical comedy, *The Masked Model*, which was to tour the country, ending up in San Francisco. The pay was seventy-five dollars a week, plus expenses.

The show closed mid-way between the two oceans, with just enough cash left to send the cast to one or other coast. Everyone except Rodolpho opted for a return to New York.

Di Valentina waved them off from the opposite platform and took the next train West for San Francisco. On his way to Hollywood.

SIX

One man with a dream, at pleasure,
Shall go forth and conquer a crown.
                              Arthur O'Shaughnessy (1844–81)

TO HIS COMPLETE mortification, Rodolpho di Valentina discovered that his name was utterly unknown in San Francisco.

The doleful Italian barman in a bay area saloon frequented by the town's theatrical set predicted he would find it easier getting employment on one of the Californian vineyards than landing himself a job in showbusiness.

But again his luck held. A young singer, who had warbled Irving Berlin's wartime hit 'Oh How I Hate To Get Up In The Morning' to a disinterested crowd of drinkers, tipped him off that a chorus job was going in the Bronson Baldwin musical *Nobody Home*.

The following morning Rodolpho auditioned for the chorus line vacancy and joined the company that night. Three weeks later the show folded. But it had served its purpose. Lunchtime socialising with other members of the cast had brought him into contact with members of a motion picture company from Hollywood who were filming on location in San Francisco.

One of them was Norman Kerry, who was already making a name for himself as an actor in the new branch of the entertainment industry. He was about the same age as the handsome young Italian, and they struck up an immediate friendship.

Kerry enthused about Rodolpho's looks and personality—the greatest assets an actor could have, he said, when breaking into the movie business—and if Rodolpho could arrange his passage to Los Angeles, he promised him a warm welcome, a place to stay and introductions to the studios. Rodolpho became very excited. The picture painted by his new friend was one of easy living and huge rewards from success in a job where repetition of short, simple-to-learn scenes could remove any mistakes a beginner might make.

He ignored Kerry's warning that Hollywood could also bring great disappointments and a possible miserable future of walk-on parts, which would scarcely pay enough to keep him above the breadline.

Two weeks later he managed to secure a free berth on the Los Angeles train with the team from the Al Jolson production *The Passing Show*.

With wonderful dreams filling his mind, he sped southwards towards the dream-makers' capital, unaware that nightmare days were once more just around the corner.

SEVEN

I wish my deadly foe no worse
Than want of friends, and empty purse
                    Nicholas Breton (1545?–1626?)

ALMOST EXACTLY FOUR years after his arrival in America,
Rodolpho di Valentina stepped off the San Francisco–
Los Angeles sleeper with all his belongings—chiefly a
suit, three spare shirts, two pairs of socks, two pairs of
underpants, cheap cologne and a toilet set—stuffed into a
bulging second-hand suitcase.

Together with the clothes he was wearing, they repre-
sented the full extent of the rewards he had managed to
accumulate since he arrived on the *Cleveland* from Italy.
In fact, he had arrived in America with more.

A few words from Al Jolson, said with a total lack of
sincerity and without the accompaniment of a smile, to
the effect that a glittering future could await him in
motion pictures, had cheered him considerably, but he
wondered if this was not yet another journey to disaster
and disappointments.

He thought again of the bridge over New York's East
river and of the night he had come close to ending his
life. If the next four years were to bring as little as the
years just past, it might be better to hurl himself now
under the wheels of the next locomotive to clank its way
through Los Angeles station.

A shout from beyond the ticket barrier interrupted his

morbid ponderings and he looked up at the grinning face of Norman Kerry, waving above a sea of heads. They shook hands warmly, and Kerry took Rodolpho's case and guided him to the street, where a gleaming new four-door Ford saloon was parked.

'Jump in,' he said. 'And we'll get you home.' He raised his fingers to his mouth as Rodolpho began to speak. 'And no damned protests,' he laughed. 'You're staying with me and that's all there is to it. If you want to break into pictures, you're going to have a decent place to sleep, a good address and someone to keep your things pressed. I have a small suite with a double room at the Alexandria Hotel and if you don't object to sharing, then I sure as hell don't.'

For the first time in his life, Rodolpho found himself speechless, unable to properly thank Kerry, who drove on in silence until they reached the outskirts of Holly-wood.

'Well, this is it,' he said, taking in with a sweep of his hand a collection of ramshackle studio buildings, restaurants, shops and hotels. 'It offers the nearest thing to instant fame and riches in the world. If you've got half the talent we think you've got, then some of that is going to be yours pretty soon.'

It was a comment Rodolpho was to recall and sneer at increasingly in the weeks that followed. Norman Kerry kept his word and he was introduced to dozens of directors, producers and agents, but none could hold out even the slightest prospect of him getting a part in a picture.

Some of the men and women he met had even heard of his reputation as a dancer back in New York, and their advice to him was to get back to dancing. He might pick up the odd job as an extra if dark-skinned heavies were

The earliest known picture of Valentino – as a moustached unknown in Italy.

Despite the middle-aged pose, this is a rare shot of the young Rudy.

Pola Negri: 'Valentino was the greatest love of my life.'

With Alice Terry, Valentino dances his famous tango to music from an early gramophone.

Jean Acker, Valentino's first wife. The marriage was a disaster.

The second Mrs Valentino – Natacha Rambova.

Above Just Married – Rudy and Natacha in Mexicali, Mexico. But he already had a wife. *Below* The Valentinos prepare for Christmas, 1922.

Natacha.

ever needed, but as for landing a leading role, forget it. He didn't have what it took, the clean American applepie good looks, to make an impact on the ladies.

With his meagre savings rapidly running out, Rodolpho was reduced to joining the other thousands of hopefuls who queued daily outside the major studios for bit parts. The man who had once had some of the most beautiful girls in New York queuing up to dance with him at ten dollars a time now had himself to suffer the ignominy of standing in line hoping to be noticed, all just to earn a miserable five dollars a day.

As the weeks ran into months, not a single offer of work as an extra had come his way. 'It's useless, nobody wants me,' he protested to Norman Kerry, the trader's son turned actor who most days was able to smuggle him into the studio canteen for a cheap meal. He ate there so frequently that many of the regulars at the studio believed he was a full-time actor.

Twice, in despair, he gave up the search for film work and took jobs dancing in some of Los Angeles's more dubious cafes. Embarrassment and poverty drove him from Norman Kerry and the Alexandria Hotel to a small room over a cafe in Santa Monica. Meagre wages and the small tips he earned as a legitimate dance instructor forced him once again to accommodate some of his female customers for afternoon sessions in his room. Most complained about their husbands, their children and the smallness of Rodolpho's ancient and unsteady single bed.

'Downstairs they pay to jump on me, and upstairs they pay for me to jump on them,' he complained, but his employers were totally lacking in sympathy. At the age of twenty-two, Rodolpho seemed destined to live out his days in California as a low-grade male prostitute.

His spirit battered, his ambition in tatters and his self-respect auctioned at ten dollar afternoon sessions in the café's upstairs room, he almost refused, then almost wept with gratitude, when Norman Kerry found him and urged him to have one more try in pictures.

An old friend, Emmett Flynn, was making a picture for First National and looking for a dancer to work as an extra. 'It could be just the break you need,' Kerry told him. At least it would take him away from the seedy life he had gradually sunk to in Santa Monica.

Rodolpho agreed to give it a try, and to his amazement Emmett Flynn, who worked as an independent director, took an almost immediate liking to him and gave him the part on the spot. His debut on the screen lasted only a few seconds, and in the studio he never even got to meet the star of *Alimony*, Josephine Whittel. But once he had seen his face on film, Rodolpho di Valentina was hooked.

Even the pitiful five dollars a day he received as an extra could not dampen his enthusiasm. In those brief moments in front of the cameras he had experienced an almost climactic thrill, which repeated itself when he watched the finished film on the screen.

To describe the film as mediocre would be to flatter it unduly. But to Rodolpho it was a minor miracle. He felt it had transformed his whole life and he determined, no matter what the obstacles, to one day become a real star.

His part in *Alimony* may have impressed him, but no-one else to whom he mentioned it remembered seeing his brief appearance in the film. So, broke again, and after further weeks of tramping from studio to studio without success, he was forced once more to take up dancing to earn a living.

This time, though, he had the promise that Emmett and *Alimony* author Hayden Talbot would seek him out

50

when the script for their next picture together was finished.

Feeling himself slipping back towards the twilight world of the afternoon dance sham, Rodolpho decided there would be no more sordid sessions in seedy bedrooms in Santa Monica. But, despite his promises to himself, when Baron Long offered him a dancing job at his newly-opened Watts Tavern on the outskirts of Los Angeles, he didn't hesitate.

The pay was only thirty-five dollars a week, but he needed the money desperately. It was comforting, too, to find that the girl who would partner him, Marjorie Tain, was also an actress fallen on hard times. She told him Watts Tavern was rapidly becoming a favourite haunt of Hollywood producers and directors, but though they danced themselves almost to a standstill five times an evening, no-one from Hollywood appeared to even notice their existence.

One night as he left the tavern, exhausted and miserable, he was seized by a highly-excited Emmett Flynn. The laughing director half dragged the confused Italian along the pavement towards a waiting car: 'I've been looking for you for a week,' he said. 'Why the hell didn't you tell anyone where you were working?'

'Would you, in my position?' asked di Valentina. 'Why, what's all this about?'

Hayden Talbot had finished the script and had tailor-written one of the main parts for him, the cheery director told him. 'You will play a really nasty piece of work. An Italian count.'

All signs of lethargy vanished. Rodolpho let rip a great cowboy yippee and performed a high-kicking leap which carried him almost on to the bonnet of Flynn's battered limousine.

Armed with a copy of the script for *The Married Virgin*, he went home and spent an almost sleepless night reading and re-reading his part. The following morning he accompanied Flynn to the production supervisor's office and walked out with a contract for fifty dollars a week.

Convinced this was his stairway to instant stardom, young di Valentina was meticulous in putting every minute detail of Flynn's direction into his performance. But once again fate, this time in the form of a camera crew dispute over money, worked against him. The picture was shelved for almost a year while financial squabbles with the production team and backers were sorted out.

In near-desperation, Rodolpho began yet another round of the Hollywood studios. He had stood in line so often, hoping for bit parts, that by now he was able to recognise several of his competitors for the hungrily sought-after scraps at the casting office windows.

Two of them, Beatrice Joy and Ramon Navarro—the man destined to become his successor almost a decade later—urged him to take a part-time job at the J. Francis Smith school of art and design on Los Angeles's Main Street.

The pair of them were modelling for the students' life classes at night and chasing film bit parts during the day. But to Rodolpho this seemed even more immoral than selling himself to the frustrated West Coast wives who were haunting habituees of the afternoon prod and pant sessions.

If he had to strip at all, he would rather do it in front of one woman who had paid for his sexual services than in front of a group of degenerate art students, most of whom he considered pansies. He was disturbingly aware of the way in which certain men in Hollywood had eyed his dancer's body and striking looks and detested the idea of even being considered a possible target for their perversions.

Nursing his bitter disappointment, he agreed to a job at the Vernon Club, an off-beat dance joint beyond the lower end of downtown Los Angeles, which was nevertheless popular with the Hollywood social set, who liked to appear daring by frequenting carefully-selected places of ill-repute.

Here there were no fancy titles handed out to the dance instructors and demonstrators. They were gigolos pure and simple. They knew it, the management knew it and the customers knew it.

As he danced, Rodolpho was half longing that someone from the film company would be attracted to him and offer him work—and half fearful that he would be recognised by someone he knew and lose all chance of further parts.

One night, as he was earning two dollars for an hour's savaging by a large, sweaty and heavily-painted society woman, who kept reaching in an embarassingly obvious manner for his more personal regions, director Bob Leonard walked in with his wife, Mae Murray, one of the most popular film stars in America.

As the couple were guided to their table, accompanied by a group of Hollywood friends, he wrenched the insistent, clutching hand of his dancing partner above waist height and hissed: 'You paid to dance. So dance, damn you, dance!'

With ramrod back and the mocking smile and smouldering look he had practised so often before the mirror, Rodolpho whirled his befuddled partner across the tiny dance floor and began working his way back and forth in

53

front of the star's table.

Twice his eyes caught those of Mae Murray, and a fierce surge of hope flooded his body as he saw her turn to a companion and, nodding in his direction, say something.

Had he been able to hear the man's reply he might not have felt so optimistic: 'He's an Italian gigolo called di Valentina. Charges two bucks an hour to be pawed by the dames and puts out to some of them back in his room.'

The vivacious young actress's eyes gleamed. 'He looks all right to me,' she said. 'What do you think, Bob?' she asked her husband. 'The guy with the slicked back hair looks okay. And a good dancer too.'

'Well, Mae,' he said, smiling indulgently at his wife. 'If that's what you think, I'll go and get him for you.'

He made his way across the floor and tapped the dancer on the shoulder. 'If you've got a moment, my wife would like to dance with you,' he said.

'I'd be delighted,' said Rodolpho, and, after hurriedly making an excuse to his partner and pushing her towards a table, he followed Leonard back across the floor.

After smiles, and a brief and casual introduction, he found himself with Mae Murray in his arms and the focus of attention for everyone in the club. It was an exhilarating moment. For here was something he could excel at. On the dance floor, he knew, few men in the country could rival him.

At the end of five minutes, a little out of breath but completely captivated, Mae Murray was full of compliments. 'You must be a professional,' she said.

'I used to be,' he explained. 'But now I'm working in pictures. I like to come here to keep myself up to scratch.'

54

The young star smiled, not letting him realise that she already knew his real reason for being in the Vernon. 'Perhaps when I come here again I'll be lucky enough to find you here,' she told him.

In the following two months Mae and Bob Leonard became regular visitors to the club. At first Rodolpho was simply invited to dance with the director's wife. But soon he was being invited to join their table and even asked to accompany them to some of the more informal Hollywood get-togethers.

Then, thanks to Emmett Flynn, he was able to quit his job at the Vernon—though he still went there to dance—and to tell his new friends, truthfully, that he was appearing in another film.

What he didn't say was that the part was that of an Italian Bowery tough and his scenes were completed in less than two days of shooting. Despite this Emmett Flynn, who was proving to be a truly sincere foul-weather friend, kept him on the payroll for the full production at the standard extra's fee of seven-and-a-half dollars a day. With this regular cash he was able to get himself new clothes and stand his turn buying drinks for his new friends Bob Leonard and Mae Murray.

Hollywood in 1918 was rather like a gold strike town of four decades earlier, just beginning to blossom from a hotch-potch of studio buildings, hastily erected restaurants and shops and a handful of hotels. The community was small and nearly everyone in the film industry knew everyone else—at least everyone else who mattered. Rodolpho was determined to get himself on the list of the latter.

The most popular eating place among many of the acting fraternity was Branstatters, and lunchtimes would see a steady parade of film people, most of them in full costume and wearing make-up, strolling from the studios along Hollywood Boulevard to the restaurant.

The main dining room was upstairs and the food was so good that some of the biggest names in the cinema would queue on the stairs to take their turn at one of the tables.

On Wednesdays and Saturdays the stars would turn out en masse for the regular dance nights. The mid-week shindig would take place at the Hollywood Hotel, which many of the big names in the industry called home. And on Saturdays they would descend on their favourite week-end haunt, the Ship's Café in Santa Monica.

Rodolpho di Valentina became a regular client at all three in addition to the Alexandria Hotel, carefully positioning himself on the edge of important groups, ready to smile and join in if his opinion were asked, or swiftly moving away if someone appeared to be about to challenge his right to be there.

He was impressed by the way in which the big earners splashed their money around. That was the Hollywood tradition, to make a lot and spend a lot, and Rodolpho swore that if he ever achieved the astronomical earnings of these legendary stars, he would outspend them all. Equally, he declared that he would never become dependent on drink as many of the most famous personalities of the day appeared to have done: one star told him he had trembled so much on the set after a night on the town that he had to have his arm wired to stop it shaking while he was being filmed with a glass in his hand.

Despite his regular attendances at all the main Hollywood watering holes, Rodolpho was unable to attract the attention of any of the better-known directors. Or even the attention of the directors who, like he, were them-

56

selves 'showing themselves about' in the hope of attracting work.

Inevitably in the end it was a woman who provided him with his first real break. Over the months Mae Murray had become increasingly involved with the one-time gigolo. But, fearful of her reputation and the unpredictable temper of her fiercely jealous husband, she had not dared suggest a private meeting with the hot-eyed, deliciously arrogant Latin.

That keenness to have him take her in his arms for purposes other than whisking her around a dance floor won him his first big role. The volatile blonde star was one of the biggest box-office earners in the world, and what she wanted she got.

What she wanted was Rodolpho di Valentina and, in almost a repeat of their first meeting, she sent husband Bob Leonard to fetch him. Reluctantly, for his suspicions of the dancer's attraction for his wife were already aroused, Leonard telephoned him and offered him the part of leading man in Mae's new picture, *The Big Little Person*.

It was clear to the whole cast and production team, as well as to the director, that Mae was putting a great deal more into the love scenes with the new boy than she usually did. Some of the kisses were so passionate that the couple's fellow actors were afraid to catch Bob Leonard's eye. Even Rodolpho seemed nervous of facing the director after one or two of his more scorching scenes with Mae. During one of them he appeared to get completely carried away and his hands began freely roaming her body. Many of his leading ladies were to experience this kind of physical proof of his arousal, but none of them, including Mae Murray, complained.

Indeed, she appeared to enjoy the experience so much

57

that she demanded he be used again in her next film, *The Delicious Little Devil*. She would play a luscious night club dancer and he the son of an Irish millionaire. More important to Rodolpho, he would be getting a hundred dollars a week and his name would go on the placards second only to that of Mae Murray herself.

The love scenes in their second picture together were, if anything, even more hot-blooded than in the first, and although Bob Leonard's professional poise appeared to be unaffected by his wife's obvious enthusiasm for the lips and caresses of her new leading man, studio gossips predicted there would not be a third film involving these two.

Whatever the reasons, they were right. But the boost to Rodolpho's career prospects had already been given. He was, as they say, on the way.

EIGHT

They told me you had been to her
And mentioned me to him:
She gave me a good character,
But I said I could not swim

Lewis Carroll (1832–98)

FOR THE FIRST time, Rodolpho di Valentina felt, instinctively, that he was on the brink of his first real success, and to meet it he decided he must have a dramatic change of personality.

From now the gregarious, eager-to-please hanger-on of his first Hollywood year would disappear for ever, to be replaced by a completely new model: a loner who would shun the crowd and thereby stand out as someone special, someone different from the rest.

As a first step towards this new image, he bought a pair of Russian wolfhounds (white) and a bathing costume (also white) and at weekends, when the majority of people from the film colony gathered on the beaches of Santa Monica, he would stroll along the sands, alone except for the two dogs. People, he noticed, would point at him and whisper his name, the men with laughter or envy, the women often wistfully or with interest. Whatever they said did not worry him. The only thing that mattered was that they were saying *something* about him.

One man who, surprisingly, said something of great

benefit was Bob Leonard. Unable, or unwilling to use Rodolpho again, he recommended the young actor to Paul Powell, who was about to direct a picture with teen-age star Carmel Meyers for Universal.

Girls often became stars at thirteen or fourteen and were finished by the time they reached eighteen, and Carmel Meyers was fifteen and di Valentina twenty-three when they made their first picture together. It was called *A Society Sensation*, and Rodolpho was paid one hundred dollars a week—only fifty a week less than his young co-star.

They met on the first day's shooting when he was brought on to the set by Paul Powell, and Carmel was bowled over by his quiet charm and staggeringly good looks. In her rest room at the studio, she told her dresser: 'He is wonderful. What style he has—and what personality. There is something about him I just can't explain. I guess it's sex. His voice is beautiful and deep, without an accent. When he said I reminded him of his people, everything fluttered inside.'

The following morning it was the turn of Rodolpho to have butterflies in his stomach when he was told that a scene of the film, being shot on location that day, called for him to rescue Carmel from the sea.

It was grey and overcast and a biting wind blew in off the Pacific on the lonely stretch of coast near Santa Monica. Carmel was in the water, clinging to rocks under a disused wharf and the director and camera crew were almost overhead.

'Okay Rudy,' Powell shouted through his megaphone. 'You run down to the pier and as soon as you see Carmel, jump into the water.'

The clapperboard snapped shut and Powell yelled 'Action!' Wearing only a brief swimming costume, Rodolpho ran on to the pier, his eyes searching the water. Pretending to catch sight of the young heroine, he registered great concern. And froze.

'Cut!' shouted Powell. 'No, Rudy—I don't want you to pause. I want you straight in. Let's do it again.'

Again Rodolpho acted the part perfectly until the moment came to jump. Once again he froze. Powell's anger began to show as he screamed again for the cameras to cut.

After a third attempt at the scene failed, Carmel's mother, who never left the unit when her daughter was filming, began complaining that her girl was in danger of catching pneumonia if she wasn't soon hauled out of the water.

By this time the director was furious: 'We'll give it one more try,' he warned di Valentina. 'Then we'll pack up and start looking for a replacement.'

Looking totally unhappy, Rodolpho returned to his position on shore. 'It will be all right this time,' he promised.

'I sincerely hope so,' snapped Powell. 'Everybody ready? Action!'

For the fourth time Rodolpho went through the pretence of spotting the now-shivering figure of Carmel in the waves. This time he didn't hesitate and leapt into the water beside her. Immediately it became apparent to everyone why he had been so reluctant to go through with the scene. He couldn't swim.

As the nearest to him, Carmel struck out, grabbed him round the chest, and hauled him into the shallow water. 'What happened?' she gasped. 'I'm a dancer—not a swimmer,' panted the shivering Rodolpho. 'I thought everybody knew that.'

From then they became good friends, and the on-screen romance between them might have blossomed off-screen, despite Carmel's youth, if it had not been for the ever-watchful eye of Mrs. Meyers.

A few days after the life-saving incident, Rodolpho called on Carmel in her dressing room. Turning to her mother, he clicked his heels, bowed, and asked: 'Madame Meyers. May I have the honour of taking your daughter out to dinner?'

'I'm very sorry, Mr. di Valentina,' she told him sternly. 'Carmel is much too young for that sort of thing.'

Completely unabashed, he pressed on: 'Madame Meyers. When I want something I don't usually let anything stand in my way.'

It was said with great charm, and great conviction, and Carmel, flattered and impressed by the Italian's words and manner, yet not daring to intervene, looked from her leading man to her mother.

'Even when what is standing in your way weighs two hundred pounds?' asked Mrs. Meyers. She smiled and Rodolpho laughed.

'Touché, Madame,' he said.

Regretfully Carmel later confided to a friend: 'I'd have loved to go out with him, or have him back to the house, or for dinner, or for anything else you might like to imagine along the way. What a pity I'm too young.'

But she did try to do everything she could to help her latest leading man—even to the extent of going to Universal chief Carl Laemmle and pleading with him to put di Valentina under contract.

Carmel, slightly taller than the affable five-feet-two-inch chief executive—who was known to all Hollywood as 'Uncle Carl'—listed Rodolpho's qualities: 'He's going to be a big star. Grab him quick, and put him under contract.'

Laemmle patted her on the back. 'Don't worry about him, girl,' he said. 'We will always be able to get him at the same price—and anyway, I'm sure he's not going to become a great star like you.'

Laemmle did, however, like the finished product of *A Society Sensation* and agreed with Powell that di Valentina be employed to do a second picture with Carmel. He even went back on his own judgment and sanctioned a wage raise which brought Rodolpho's earnings up to 125 dollars a week.

Convinced by this new recognition of his talent that he had finally won a place for himself among the regularly employed, and wishing to further his new dashing image, Rodolpho rushed out and put a down-payment on a huge Mercer automobile, agreeing to pay the balance of 750 dollars by monthly cheques of 50 dollars.

He spent all his spare time off the set of *All Night* in his car or under it, for the second-hand giant frequently broke down. He was a very fast, but not very good, driver and other motorists in Hollywood soon learned to pull over when they heard the roaring engine of the Mercer overhauling them.

In the cut-out open seat, and accompanied by a constantly changing stream of beautiful companions, Rodolpho was aware he cut a splendid figure. He had a flair for drawing attention to himself, a natural showman who boasted to Norman Kerry: 'It won't be long before everyone will be saying: "There goes di Valentina" whenever I appear in public. Even though no-one will know the *real* me.'

But the completion of his second picture with Carmel Meyers brought yet another reversal of his fortunes. After playing the second lead in four consecutive films he had, not unnaturally, assumed that his worth as an actor

63

had been recognised in Hollywood, and it was hard for him to accept the bit parts in a string of pictures which were all that were offered to him in the following six months.

One of the first casualties was the Mercer. Reduced again to fifty-dollars-a-part roles, he could not keep up the monthly payments and the finance company took away the car. He claimed that repair bills had cost more than the actual payments and that he was glad to see the back of it, but it hurt his ego not to be able to drive down Hollywood Boulevard in his gleaming success symbol. Girls, too, he noticed, were less willing to join him when he had no car. And, on top of all his other problems, he became very ill.

The worst Spanish influenza epidemic since the turn of the century had swept through California earlier in the year, and though many of the film and dance-hall people he knew had been stricken with it, he had come through unscathed.

He put it down to his tough Italian boyhood and the daily sessions of exercises and calesthenics with which he greeted each morning. Perhaps, friends thought, that was true—he had been eating badly because of his straitened circumstances and few people in his position managed to resist the bug for as long as he did.

When he did catch it, he got it badly. But even after six years in America, Rodolpho still retained the peasants' fear of doctors. Though his temperature soared to 104, and the fever raged day after day, he refused to see a physician or take medicines. 'I don't believe in doctors,' he told friends through cracked and burning lips. 'I am strong enough to fight any illness unaided.' They were words those friends would remember and recall with sadness in the years ahead.

Recovered, he was forced to turn again to Norman Kerry, his closest friend in Hollywood, for help. And Kerry, as always, was ready with a bed and a handout to tide him over. Despite opposition from the director, he even managed to work Rodolpho into *Virtuous Sinners*, the picture in which he himself was appearing, but his friend's footage ended mainly on the cutting room floor and he was barely noticeable in the background in the finished version.

The part as a heavy to Dorothy Gish in a picture being made by the already legendary D. W. Griffith temporarily resurrected di Valentina's hopes of stardom, but on completion the director told him the only re-booking he would get would be as a stage dancer doing the live prologues to Griffith's future productions.

In no position to turn down the one hundred dollars a week offered, he agreed to team up with Griffith's latest protégé and 'companion' Carol Dempster, dancing the prologue to *The Greatest Thing in Life,* which featured three months at the Auditorium Theatre in Los Angeles.

During this highly-successful engagement, he auditioned with Griffith for the part of the Mexican hero in *Scarlet Days* and for more than a week spent hours into every night after leaving the theatre studying the script. It was a bitter disappointment when he lost the part to Richard Barthelmess.

The main reason, Griffith told him, was that Barthelmess showed a great deal more restraint in his acting of the character, and if Rodolpho could do less arm-waving and facial contortions, and learn to express himself with eyes and mouth in a less obvious fashion, his acting career would stand slightly more chance of getting off the ground. Never slow to accept advice if the person dishing it out was an expert, he took the director's words to heart and began putting these suggestions into practice during long sessions in front of a bedroom mirror.

His disappointment in failing to get the part was made even more difficult to swallow when Griffith offered him the job of dancing in the prologue to *Scarlet Days*. Simply to warm up the audience for the star he felt he should have been almost reduced Rodolpho to tears. But for one hundred dollars a week he was prepared to do almost anything that would stop him returning to his old standby work as a dance hall gigolo. At least this way he was working for one of the major studios, even if not on film.

Shelved, too, for the time being at any rate, was his carefully-nurtured new image as a loner. Without work in pictures, and with the possibility of stardom pushed once more into the far distance, he needed regular contact with more of the people who might recognise his talent and find him employment as an actor. And for this he relied on friends like Norman Kerry and actor-turned-director Douglas Gerrard, whom he had known for most of his two years in Hollywood.

They were the friends who stood by him and consoled him at his most despairing point—when a letter arrived from Italy with the news he had dreaded. His mother had died. He wept bitterly, knowing now that he could never prove to her what a success he could be. Filled with remorse, he thought of giving up this life and returning to Italy for her funeral, perhaps for ever. But his persistent problem, a severe lack of funds, made even that impossible, and he could only pray that his mother, at the end, had remembered him with love.

Now, desperate for recognition, to prove himself a success if only as a posthumous offering to his mother, he hesitated to turn down any invitation which might involve a meeting with one of the powerful studio bosses or directors, and it was this urgent need which persuaded him to accept a casual invitation to a small dinner party being held at the Ship's Café.

It came during a chance meeting with composer-conductor's daughter Dagmar Godowsky, whom he had met in New York while exhibition dancing in the clubs.

She had been asked to the party to celebrate the completion of Nazimova's latest picture, *Stronger Than Death*, and understood that several Metro bigwigs would be there, including one of the important studio managers, Maxwell Karger.

It was too great an opportunity to miss, and Rodolpho promised to join Dagmar in the Santa Monica restaurant that evening. Hurrying home, he took out his best suit and, after half a dozen unsuccessful phone calls, located a friend who would lend him a car to take him on the journey to the coast.

When he arrived, about twenty people were already seated at the large table. He checked his appearance in a mirror by the door and set his face in a warm smile before striding across the room to join them. Maxwell Karger had just proposed a toast to the Russian star and everyone had their glasses raised as Rodolpho reached the table and caught Dagmar Godowsky's eye. She smiled and beckoned him round and started to introduce him. Then Nazimova caught sight of the newcomer.

The beautiful young actress who had invited him remembered later: 'She lowered her head and froze. Her little frame was rigid and she looked as though she were having a divine fit. The whole table took its cue from her and one by one they, too, lowered their heads in this shocking form of grace. My voice tailed off, and so did his.'

Nazimova broke the tableau and thundered: 'How dare you bring that gigolo to my table? How dare you introduce that pimp to Nazimova?'

Everyone at the table was shocked into silence. Not a glass chinked and not a person moved as Rodolpho, face burning and eyes flooding, almost ran from the restaurant.

With no attempt to hide her sniggers, Nazimova recounted how Rodolpho had been at the centre of an unsavoury scandal in New York which ended with Bianca de Saulles slaying her husband. Most of the guests knew that Bianca had murdered her husband over custody of their child and had been acquitted at her trial, but no-one chose to challenge the Russian's interpretation of the two-year-old events.

Nazimova's terrible insult to the good-looking young actor had distressed a number of the people at the table, however, and one of them, an attractive, dark-haired young Metro starlet called Jean Acker, was almost in tears when she asked to be excused from the rest of the party.

Dagmar Godowsky also offered her bleak excuses and walked away. Within five minutes, the dinner party had broken up and Nazimova, deeply regretting her hasty display of dramatics, was left to return to her home alone.

Unaware of this demonstration of sympathy for the churlish treatment he had been subjected to, Rodolpho drove home to his Hollywood apartment in tears of self-pity and shame. He felt that the story of his disgrace would sweep the town and he would never again dare venture out.

Again he found himself wrestling with the temptation to put an end to his life, but the thought that he would be condemning himself for someone else's injustice stayed his hand.

Finally it was Douglas Gerrard who came to the rescue. As Rodolpho had feared, the story had been repeated throughout Hollywood—but far from laughing at him, the whole community was outraged by Nazimova's infamous conduct.

Actress Pauline Frederick, he revealed, had heard about the incident and was waiting at the Los Angeles Athletic Club bar to invite Rodolpho to a party at her sumptuous, newly-built mansion on Sunset Boulevard.

It was, as it turned out, an invitation to disaster.

NINE

Marriage is like life in this
That it is a field of battle, and not a bed of roses.

Robert Louis Stevenson (1850–94)

IRONICALLY IT WAS Jean Acker—who had shed tears on Rodolpho's behalf when she feared he would become a laughing stock—who would become responsible for making him the subject of ridicule and the pathetic butt of a host of cruel Hollywood jokes.

Had he been able to foresee the result of going to Pauline Frederick's party, it is doubtful if he would have ventured within many miles of her home that Sunday.

But the rudeness of Nazimova, and lingering grief over his mother's death, made the emotional Rodolpho more than usually susceptible to a sympathetic companion, and when Pauline introduced him to Jean Acker and explained her distress on his behalf, he was deeply affected.

He noted that Jean Acker favoured a short, very masculine hairstyle, and wore a white blouse and tie under a rather severely cut suit, but it did not occur to him that the instant friendship which blossomed between them could just as easily have been of the type which can spring up between two compatible men.

He had heard rumours that Nazimova maintained a circle of attractive young women of sapphist inclination for her personal amusement and pleasure, but he was not then aware that Jean Acker's more intimate friendships

70

were also reserved for women. It amused some of the other party guests to see the man who was so openly and fiercely proud of his virility and masculinity courting such a romantically improbable woman. Perhaps they thought he knew of the stories about her or perhaps they delighted in seeing the arrogant, self-opinionated foreigner so hopelessly off course.

Rodolpho was, in fact, enjoying her company. He found her totally lacking in coquettishness and devoid of the fluttering-eyed insincerity of most Hollywood actresses. Their friendship had got off to such a promising start that he was eager to develop it further. For Rodolpho that meant a more private venue where he could demonstrate a more physical appreciation of the actress's effect on him.

Never slow when it came to exploiting a romantic situation, and unused to holding back his totally basic and barely-concealed passions, he insisted on arranging another, more intimate, meeting. But the petite, hazel-eyed starlet carefully side-stepped his heavily-insinuated invitations, agreeing only to meet him in the restaurant of the Hollywood Hotel, where she lived.

An apartment at the Hollywood Hotel was a far cry from his couple of rooms on the poorer side of La Cienega, but Rodolpho was unabashed. 'I was already falling in love with this charming and beautiful young woman,' he said later. 'Even before I met her next day, I knew that I wanted her for my wife.'

A few days after their meeting in the restaurant, convinced that he had found the woman who would be his life's soulmate, Rodolpho committed some of his few remaining dollars to hiring a pair of horses and invited Jean Acker for a ride in the moonlight.

Judging by what happened next, his plan was a run-

71

away success. As they headed downhill from the ridge above Beverly Hills, Jean Acker gazed at the moonlight filtering through the branches of the tall trees and stretched lazily in the saddle.

'Isn't this romantic?' she said.

'Yes, but wouldn't it be more so if we rode to Santa Ana and got married?' he suggested.

She looked up, startled. 'You'd better not be serious about that, or I'll take you up.'

'I am serious,' he replied.

Twenty minutes later when they reached her hotel, these casual exchanges had hardened into a definite re-solve to marry. There would be no waiting period—a tragic error on both parts—but they would marry by special licence the following day.

In the hotel they bumped into Maxwell Karger and his wife, who told them a party was being given the fol-lowing evening for Richard Rowland, the Metro presi-dent, and his wife, who were returning to New York. If the couple were serious about getting married, the party could double as a wedding celebration.

Next morning Rodolpho got the special licence and that evening they were married. At the party, Rodolpho had two announcements to make. Although everyone knew him as Rodolpho di Valentina, he had married Jean Acker in his real name of Guglielmi. But henceforth he had decided, in deference to his new wife's suggestion, he would be known as Rudolph Valentino.

'Sounds a bit like the Holy Trinity,' yelled one guest. 'Which name shall we toast?'

'All three,' laughed the new 'Rudolph'. 'But when you see my name in lights, it will be as Rudolph Valen-tino.'

Shortly before midnight the couple drove in a borrowed car towards the Hollywood Hotel, in preference to Rudolph's dingy apartment.

Valentino was almost beside himself with impatience to taste the delights which he had no doubt his beautiful young bride was just as eager to bestow on him.

They had left the party hand in hand and now they were just a few paces away from the welcoming privacy of Jean's apartment. The 5ft 11in Italian was almost dragging the diminutive actress by the time they reached the hotel lobby.

'Slow down,' she said. 'You don't give a girl time to think.'

'This is no time for thinking,' smiled Rudolph. 'This is a time for action' and, placing his arm around her waist, he almost swept her the last few feet to the door of her ground-floor rooms.

At the back of the hotel a small group of actors and actresses, who had dashed ahead of the newlyweds, crouched by the slightly open window of Jean's bedroom, each clutching a tin can filled with pebbles, and ready to spring up and shake thier home-made rattles as the couple came in.

But instead of the soft, affectionate voices they had expected, they heard the cold, angry voice of Jean Acker ordering her husband of six hours to leave the hotel.

It had all been a dreadful mistake, she told him. She did not love him. Pitied him, perhaps. But loved him, never. There was no way in which she was going to allow him to touch her. The thought of his body on hers nauseated her.

Horrified, the listeners heard the bewildered, hurt bridegroom plead with her to give their marriage a try. But she refused to listen. She had been a fool, she said, to believe she could see it through.

Then she began to curse him and screamed at him to leave her apartment. She did not want him, then or ever. He could not share her bed, her room or even the hotel.

Confused and unable to fully grasp what was happening, Valentino backed from the room under her onslaught, begging her to accept his love, until finally, as though recognising his position was hopeless, he stumbled from the hotel and crossed, weeping, to the car.

Here was the ultimate mockery, the final derisive blow, a farce of such absurdity that people would still be laughing at Valentino the Hollywood joker in fifty years. To be thrown out of his bride's room on his wedding night must make a man seem the most gullible and ridiculous of God's creatures. So many triumphs in illicit affairs to his credit wiped out by his contemptible failure to consummate this lawful union.

It was dawn before Rudolph Valentino, destined to be called the world's greatest lover, the God of Love, could accept the fact that his wife had spurned him, and not even for another man.

TEN

Nay, I'll do him justice.
I'm his friend, I won't wrong him.

William Congreve (1670–1729)

ONCE AGAIN RUDOLPH turned to Norman Kerry for advice—and the advice was hardly what he expected to hear. Far from trying to persuade him to 'stick it out' in the hope that Jean might suddenly come to her senses, the young actor advised his friend: 'Get along to as many parties as possible, and go to town on the girls. You may be married, but there's no way they can accuse you of being unfaithful. You haven't had the chance to be faithful yet.'

Rudolph grinned at Kerry's straight-from-the-shoulder assessment of his marital status and promised to try to carry out his advice. Acknowledging too, that he may have been a little hasty in proposing marriage to an almost complete stranger, he assured Kerry that in future he would make his head rule his heart.

But despite his eagerness to put a brave face on his wedding night rebuttal, Rudolph found it difficult to penetrate more than a handful of Hollywood shindigs. Jean Acker, under a 200-dollars-a-week contract to Metro, was far more acceptable to the hosts of the celluloid city's pre-Christmas festivities than her hapless spouse. He found himself limited to insignificant celebrations and the regular hotel and club dances.

At least on the dance floor, he reasoned, there was little chance of him making an even bigger fool of himself, and it was on one of these occasions, at the Screen Club dance, that he met one of the big-name Metro stars, Viola Dana.

She was sitting at a large table with Jack Pickford and a group of other showbusiness friends. She had seen him dance before, and as she herself was raised as a dancer, readily accepted when he asked her to partner him for the inevitable tango.

Afterwards he escorted her back to her table and rejoined some bit-part actors with whom he had been talking—they to learn the truth about his split with Jean Acker, he to pick up any information about forthcoming films.

At her table some of Viola's companions gently chided her for so obligingly partnering Valentino: 'It's just not done to dance with that fellow,' said one of the studio executives. 'He's still little more than a gigolo.'

'I think that's rather an unkind word to use,' the young star snapped. 'So he was paid for dancing with unescorted women? Well, I don't think there's anything wrong in that. It's nice for a single girl to be able to go along and partner a beautiful dancer like him, and not have some old guy stepping all over her feet. I think it's kind of ridiculous that people are not expected to dance with him. It's probably because all the guys are jealous of him.'

Support like that, from someone he had only just met, would have done wonders for Rudolph's flagging pride if he had overheard it. But little occurred in the next few weeks to either restore his self-confidence or make him very optimistic about the future. A small part as Norman Kerry's brother—which his friend somehow managed to organise with First National—in *Passion's Playground*, was promised him for the New Year and he got through the remainder of November and December playing minor roles in *The Adventuress* and *The Cheater*, a Henry Otto-directed picture in which he played the villain. This was filmed at Metro, where the dressing rooms for the cast of various pictures were sited together in one part of the studio.

One of them was occupied by Viola Dana, and he caught sight of her as he was leaving the studio on Christmas Eve. He rapped on the window of her bathing hut-style dressing room and called out: 'Merry Christmas!'

'Merry Christmas,' she replied. 'What are you up to tonight?'

'Well, the truth is I'm not doing anything,' he told her.

'Why, that's awful. You mean it's Christmas Eve and you haven't got a place to go?'

He shook his head.

'Well you've got some place to go now,' she said. 'Wait until I've finished dressing and you're coming home with me. I have a big house in Beverly Hills with my sister and her husband. My parents are going to be there, so it will be quite a get-together.'

She paused and stepped out of her dressing room and looked Valentino up and down. 'You'll do fine,' she said.

'For what?'

'As the leading man in our Christmas fun and games,' she told him. 'I want you to play Santa Claus.'

That role gave Rudolph Valentino more satisfaction than any of the film characterisations he was paid for in the next six months. Wearing a long red cape and sporting a white beard and moustache, he belly-laughed, ad libbed and waddled from guest to guest handing out

77

presents.

'He was delighted,' Viola said later. 'We always have extra presents in the house put aside for unexpected guests like Rudy, and we dug some out and wrapped them up for him. You'd think we'd given him some kind of treasure, the way he reacted. He couldn't get over us thinking enough of him to give him a Christmas present.

'When we found he didn't have any place to go on Christmas Day, I asked him to spend the night with us and we could have the next day all together. I could cry afterwards thinking about it, him being all alone at that time of year.'

He stayed the whole of Christmas with Viola and it did much to dispel the gloom and unhappiness of recent events—though the arrangement that he sleep in her home did little for her reputation. Not that she cared a damn: 'He needs to be with someone,' she said. 'Rudy's always been a perfect gentleman with me and I like him very much. We're just a load of kids trying to make movies. Let's at least give each other a little help.'

If friendship and open public recognition of Valentino could help, then Viola Dana was just the girl to provide it. Her parties were the envy of Los Angeles. As she said: 'When I give a party it's in order to have a hell of a lot of fun. I've given some beauts.'

One 'beaut' she gave for Winnie Sheehan, head of production at Fox studios. Sheehan and his wife, former opera star Maria Jeritza, lived in opulent style, even by Hollywood mogul standards. The former crime reporter had a million-dollar mansion in Beverly Hills and a retreat in the San Fernando valley. But even Sheehan was impressed by the party Viola organised in her home in his honour. There was an outside bar and an inside bar, with two extras in cowboy outfits guarding the con-

78

necting door. Guests who failed to down a drink at the outside bar were stopped from going any further by the gun-toting couple, who fired their weapons in the air and pointed the way back to the drink-littered counter.

Valentino, quiet, well-mannered and immaculate, was always a model guest at those parties, never intruding but always hovering within sight and earshot of any of the headliners and studio top brass. At one get-together he met Lewis Selznick, the Kiev-born jewellery salesman turned movie pioneer, who was impressed with the Italian and steered him into a film being shot on location in New York by his own production company.

Valentino would receive three hundred dollars a week for his work on *The Wonderful Chance*, in which he played a leading role alongside Eugene O'Brien and Martha Mansfield. It wasn't equal to the kind of money Mary Pickford and Charlie Chaplin were commanding—the two superstars of the early Twenties were taking a million dollars a year out of pictures—but it was well up with the second league stars.

With his luck seemingly running in full spate, Valentino found himself in demand for another New York-based movie, shooting slightly earlier than *The Wonderful Chance*, and he was signed for that too. His pay would be the same—this time for playing a heavy opposite opera star Margaret Namara in *Stolen Moments*.

Even Jean Acker's refusal to compromise over their separation failed to dampen Rudolph's spirits. He found New York slightly changed, though many of the cabarets and clubs in which he had worked four years earlier were still doing brisk business.

'When I was here last', he told his co-star, 'I found my friends among the showgirls and performers who were completely out with decent families. They would have nothing to do with me, and would not allow their daughters to have anything to do with me. But their daughters were anxious for romance and didn't pay any attention.'

He quickly set about renewing his acquaintance with as many of the 'delightful young ladies from both sides of the social fence' as made themselves available. It was a triumphant return to New York, but an even more triumphant return to Hollywood was already being decided for him.

As with all the momentous events in Valentino's life, this one was also initiated by a woman—filmland's highest-paid scriptwriter, June Mathis.

On the strength of a five-minute sequence in an already forgotten film, she had picked out Valentino to play the lead in the most important movie yet in Hollywood's history, the first million-dollar epic.

It was to be called *The Four Horsemen of the Apocalypse.*

ELEVEN

I am going in search of a great perhaps.

François Rabelais (1492–1553)

ORIGINALLY WRITTEN IN Spanish by Vicente Blasco Ibanez, *The Four Horsemen of the Apocalypse* had been translated and published in America at the end of the First World War. It was instantly acclaimed by the critics as the best novel to come out of the four-year European holocaust, and within twelve months had seen over fifty printings.

It told the story of two Argentinian sisters who were married—one to a Frenchman, the other to a German. When their father, a multi-millionaire dies, they travel to Europe and settle in their husbands' homelands.

To the Frenchman is born a son, Julio, who becomes an extravagant and colourful figure of Bohemian Paris night life. Julio has an affair with a married woman, Marguerite Laurier, who frequently joins him in the French cabarets to tango, the latest dance craze to hit Europe.

When war breaks out, Julio refuses to enlist, but when he follows Marguerite to the front, where her husband has been wounded, sight of the German atrocities changes his mind. He joins the French army, is promoted from private to lieutenant and awarded the Croix de Guerre for extreme bravery. Finally the war brings him face to face with his German cousin and as the pair join in combat a high explosive shell bursts nearby and kills them both.

The four horsemen of the Apocalypse are, of course, War, Conquest, Famine and Death.

* * *

In Hollywood Metro executives, who blamed financial difficulties in the company on the failure of its war pictures, refused to consider an offer for film rights of the book.

But in New York Metro chief Richard Rowland (whose farewell party from the West Coast had doubled as Valentino's wedding reception) was highly impressed by the book's sales figures and began negotiations with the author's agents.

After a good deal of haggling he agreed a contract for twenty thousand dollars against ten per cent of the picture's gross earnings—a deal which appalled his associates in Hollywood—and called in the woman considered to be the best scenario writer of the day, June Mathis.

Thrilled by her professional and sympathetic handling of the story, Rowland decided to trust her even further. The film would need a first-class director and a promotable leading man, both of whom should be well known to the public and the picture industry, he said.

He asked June Mathis to pick the right two men.

She ignored Rowland's advice, selected two comparative unknowns and helped to create one of Hollywood's greatest directors and its most lasting, worshipped and legendary star.

Rex Ingram, a young, dynamic and highly-creative director, was overjoyed at being chosen to capture on film the stirring and savage Ibanez best-seller, but was shaken by the selection of Rudolph Valentino as his leading man.

He was aware that Metro were sinking the largest budget in film history into the making of this epic, and that the whole future of the company rested on the success of this one picture. Casting an unknown, instead of a big name with proven box office success, seemed to Ingram a risky way of insuring Metro's future.

But he knew he owed his own presence on *The Four Horsemen* to June Mathis, and that she had endorsed his choice of his fiancée, Alice Terry, as the female lead. So he satisfied himself with a few personal and critical comments about Valentino and gracefully gave in to her choice.

June Mathis had already started work on the script of *The Four Horsemen* when she spotted Valentino. She liked to break up her efforts at the typewriter with visits to the local picture theatre, and on one of these occasions *The Eyes of Youth* was showing. Though he appeared only in the third episode opposite Clara Kimball Young, and played the part of a heavy, Valentino's performance impressed the scriptwriter. He had the looks, the arrogance and the emotion to play Julio, she decided. But before mentioning her choice to either Ingram or Rowland she obtained a copy of *The Eyes of Youth* and studied again and again Valentino's interpretation of the flashy young divorce co-respondent before finally making up her mind.

This was the only possible Julio.

The first Valentino knew of his selection was when he received a message at the New York studio where he was filming *A Wonderful Chance*. He was asked to call on Richard Rowland at Metro, and when he arrived was taken straight to Rowland's inner sanctum and introduced to June Mathis, of whom he had heard but never met.

'I'd like you to play Julio in *The Four Horsemen*,' she

told him.

Valentino looked open-mouthed from one to the other. In common with every other individual connected with the cinema, he knew Metro were planning a mammoth production of the Ibanez book and had even considered auditioning for the part. But he was not aware their plans had already reached the stage of selecting the cast.

'I'd love to play the part,' gasped Valentino, regaining the use of his voice. 'But are you sure?'

'What are you earning at present?' asked Rowland, recognising the Italian's complete vulnerability to a quick financial advantage while overwhelmed by this totally unexpected offer.

'Four hundred dollars a week,' said Valentino automatically.

'Would you be willing to take less than that?'

'Three hundred and fifty for example, to have the chance of playing Julio?' Rowland pressed home his advantage.

'Of course,' said Valentino, still slightly dazed from the suddenness of being confronted with real stardom after so many years of waiting and hoping and dreaming.

'Now you've settled the money side of things, perhaps you'd like to know why I chose you,' said June Mathis, eyes smiling behind large horn-rimmed spectacles.

Still quite unable to fully appreciate his change of luck, Valentino sat and listened with a rapt expression on his face as she extolled his attributes and miming talents. When she revealed the identity of his leading lady, he jumped to his feet, spontaneously applauding. For Alice Terry, then under her real name of Alice Taaffe, had been another extra in his first Hollywood movie, *Alimony*.

Half-an-hour later, clutching a Metro contract to

prove his unexpected good fortune, Valentino hurried back to the set of *The Wonderful Chance* and, leaping on to a chair, excitedly announced to the whole film crew that he was to be a star. The director, George Archainbaud, who had grown to like Valentino for his enthusiasm, co-operation and punctuality during filming, congratulated him on winning the plum role of this, or any other, year and promised to speed shooting of the remaining scenes in which he was scheduled to appear, so that he could leave for Hollywood at the earliest opportunity.

Two weeks later, Valentino stepped off the train in Los Angeles and experienced the first material proof of his change of status. A Metro chauffeur was waiting at the barrier to collect him and his luggage, and drive him to the Hollywood Hotel, where a small suite had been booked in his name.

At the studio, he was treated as an important actor by the other members of the cast and given a large dressing room with its own bathroom and day bed. His first visitor was June Mathis. She told him he was destined to become one of the greatest stars in Hollywood, but to ensure this he must pay scrupulous attention to the direction of Rex Ingram.

He must show great restraint in portraying the part of Julio and rely on his eyes to get across to the audience most of the character's inner feelings and emotions.

Valentino promised total obedience to her and the director and begged her to help him understand his part better by coaching him in the greatest detail with her interpretation of Julio's personality.

Every moment he was filming, June Mathis was on hand, ready to offer advice or criticism. At the same time Rex Ingram, who was determined the film should be a box-office blockbuster, spent many patient hours nursing the finest performance possible from the leading man he felt had been foisted on him.

Valentino responded to their friendly assistance by re-doubling his own efforts. He was polite to everyone connected with the picture and never once argued with Ingram who, as work continued, was gradually changing his opinion of the Italian. It was becoming evident from the daily rushes that the scenes involving Valentino were more than successful. They were incredible. At the expense of his fiancée's part, Ingram asked June Mathis to re-write the script, giving more of the story to Julio.

Even some of the hardy professionals on the film crew were roused to cheers by Valentino's tango sequences. First garbed as a gaucho in Argentina, then wearing tails as the Paris playboy, he was dancing his way into cinema history. There was nothing that even Rex Ingram's directorial skill could add to Valentino's fiery and utterly personal interpretation of the South American dance.

But in other scenes, Ingram, a perfectionist, rehearsed and re-rehearsed his actor until completely satisfied he could not extract even a fractional improvement in his performances. He alone, Ingram stated often, would be responsible if the picture were a flop. The actors could take credit if *The Four Horsemen* was a smash success, but only the director could really be blamed if it was panned by the critics.

Valentino, with unquestioning confidence in the adventurous director, prayed that the film would be the success they all needed, and endeavoured to be even more co-operative, willing and attentive both on and off the set. He was, his fellow actors agreed, one of the most easy-going but hardworking members of their profession they had ever had the pleasure of working with.

These kind words, together with the rave reviews from the editing room, were not lost on the newspaper and magazine reporters who almost daily swarmed around the studios looking for tit-bits of information and gossip about the most important movie yet filmed. Many of them began to feature the name Valentino in their stories, and several predicted that he would become a star.

It was at this point that Valentino first sketched out the fictitious background story that was to become the blueprint for biographers for almost half a century. His father, he claimed, had been a captain in one of the crack Italian cavalry regiments. When he died he was given a military funeral and his coffin transported in a coach drawn by six horses. The coachmen wore uniforms of black and silver, and his father's friends had walked beside the hearse holding large tassels.

He had also been to a top grammar school, he said, And to the Royal Military Academy. As a teenager he had travelled through France and enjoyed many amorous adventures in Paris, where he had fought a duel over a lady's honour. This, he told reporters, explained the scar on his cheek.

He had travelled to New York with a gift of four thousand dollars from his wealthy mother and there he had been Superintendent in charge of laying out Italian gardens for a millionaire's estate before taking up dancing and acting professionally.

These hastily-invented details of his early life were embroidered even more by the studio publicity writers and, as Press interest in him grew, Valentino had difficulty remembering the 'facts' about his pre-Hollywood history.

As was the pattern in his future acting, Valentino now took on the character of the part he was playing. Pleasant, philosophical and sensitive—as was Julio—he was able to recount his early adventures with remarkable conviction, and one gullible girl reporter was actually moved to tears by his heartrending account of his father's death.

A new star was in the process of being born, and Valentino was determined he should emerge with all the right social connections. Halfway through the picture, Metro executives smilingly gave their okay to complete shooting. They, too, sensed they had a surefire winner on their hands. A triple winner in fact, in the shape of Valentino, Ingram and *The Four Horsemen*.

Twelve thousand people took part in the production on sets constructed of 125,000 tons of materials, and the half million feet of film were edited to two hours running time for the theatres. Some of the symbolic scenes, with the Four Horsemen galloping across the sky, were described as truly spectacular.

Avidly, Rudolph Valentino read every comment on production printed in the Press and in magazines (especially those pieces which mentioned him) and noted that only an occasional article predicted Metro had thrown good money after bad in producing yet another war picture and questioned their wisdom in pinning their hopes on two unknown leads and a little-known director.

It would be eight months before the picture could be premiered and those predictions proved right or wrong. Meanwhile Valentino received approaches from some of the other Hollywood studios, but on June Mathis's advice agreed to make at least one more Metro film before the release of *The Four Horsemen*, which, she said, would undoubtedly dramatically change his bargaining position.

Eagerly accepting her advice—he was still plagued by debts—Valentino signed to do *Uncharted Seas*, playing the lead opposite Alice Lake. Still waiting to get the public's reaction to an Italian romantic star, Metro did not offer him more money and, quite content to be so readily employed again, Valentino did not ask for it.

The new film, a trivial account of unlikely adventures in Alaska, finished early in the New Year and found Valentino still in his Hollywood Hotel apartment, steadily running-up a new collection of creditors—including the salesman of a large and very powerful open sports car.

With regular money flowing in and his prospects bright, Valentino had also reverted to his old ideas about an image for himself as a loner. Actresses and would-be actresses, with an almost uncanny instinct for picking out men who were on their way up, now vied with one another to partner the quiet, serious and impeccably-dressed Italian. But most of their invitations went straight into his wastepaper basket.

He preferred to keep his romantic activities away from the limelight—particularly as Jean Acker, who had refused all his written appeals to return to him, was now out of work, having left Metro, and complaining that her husband was making no attempt to support her.

As sexually potent as ever, he would sneak girls into his hotel suite by a back entrance, or go to the home of one of his more discreet friends, like actress Gertrude Astor, who would invite along attractive young companions for his amusement.

'He had very few girls that anyone knew about,' said Gertrude later, 'He would come to my place and I would have a girl friend there and he would pair off with her.

'I would play the piano and we would sing a bit. He liked quiet parties, but he certainly knew what to do with a woman.'

The one woman he was not sure what to do with was Jean Acker. Living down his humiliation at being so badly treated on his wedding night, he could even contemplate the idea of marrying someone else sometime in the future. But this would first of all entail obtaining a divorce from Jean, and June Mathis, with whom he discussed the problem, as he did every other problem that beset him, advised patience. The marriage had not been consummated. Let a few more months go by and then quietly divorce her, she said.

But Jean Acker had other ideas. On January 17, 1921, Valentino was served with court papers on a suit she had filed for maintenance.

She claimed he had refused to live with her, had never supported her and had deserted her. Now she demanded three hundred dollars a month maintenance and asked for lawyers' fees totalling more than a thousand dollars.

Valentino was, in turn, shocked, consumed by fury and distraught. He bellowed with rage, wept and broke every item of crockery on a lunch trolley wheeled into his suite by a nervous waiter. How could she accuse him of desertion—he who had been dismissed from his bridal suite so ignominiously? He would confront her and give her the thrashing a true Italian husband would mete out to his wife at the first hint of disobedience.

Fortunately Valentino consulted with June Mathis and Norman Kerry before rushing off to deal with his estranged wife, and they advised caution and a visit to a lawyer.

The lawyer, in turn advised a cross-complaint for divorce, Rudolph's silence and an application to have the hearing set back at least six months. The actor had wisely kept copies of his many letters to Jean Acker, and her replies. With these, the lawyer told him, the money-hungry Mrs. Guglielmi stood very little chance of succeeding in her infamous action.

Valentino was slightly comforted, but still pessimistic about the outcome of the court case. Was it not a fact, he wailed, that on every occasion when things appeared to be looking up for him, something happened to drag him down again?

Couldn't just one thing really wonderful happen without being diluted with disaster?

In March, *The Four Horsemen of the Apocalypse* opened simultaneously in New York, Chicago and Boston and Valentino's prayed-for triumph became reality. Without exception the critics hailed it as a masterpiece and Valentino as a star. The following day, long queues formed outside all theatres where the film was playing. As the days ran into weeks, the queues grew longer.

The critics had found a star, and tens of thousands of American women had found a new heart-throb.

TWELVE

Genius is of no country; his pure ray
Spreads all abroad, as general as the day.
Charles Churchill (1731–64)

WHEN *The Four Horsemen* opened in Britain (at the
Palace Theatre in London), it was an instant success,
creating a box-office record within weeks. The *Daily
Mail* critic hailed it as 'a great advance in film production', praised the 'magnificent' photography and the
choice of 'well-marked racial types' for the cast.

Unwittingly substantiating the hoary showbusiness
dictum that actors should never appear with children or
animals, he observed: 'Even the baby crying by its dead
mother in a deserted village on the Marne, and the
amusing little monkey which appears now and again,
were clever actors.' But 'Perhaps we see rather too much
of the hero and his lady love, for at times their scenes are
so long drawn-out that the story drags.'

On the whole, though, he advised, 'it is an excellent
film. Last night it held the attention so closely that
smoking or talking was indulged in by very few of the
fashionable audience which filled the theatre.'

Within days, audiences were not given the opportunity
to talk even during the four-minute interval: the League
of Nations Union, mightily impressed by the film's
propaganda potential, contacted presenter Marcus Loew,

and asked if its officials could make speeches 'short enough not to be resented by the public' halfway through the showings.

Mr. Loew, mightily impressed himself, not only agreed that speakers could press home the film's lessons, but shortly afterwards announced that he was ready to send a copy of *The Four Horsemen* to Geneva, where the Assembly of the League of Nations was sitting.

Representatives of the 50 nations could make use of it in their countries, he said, and apart from any idea of profits or losses concerned, he was willing to send more copies of the film, at his own expense, to more remote parts so that peoples who had not been 'in personal touch with the Great War' might realise something of what it meant to those who had.

All this, and the film's immense success, did not please the German government. Their Ambassador in Rome, it was revealed, had been told to request the Italian government to ban its showing. But the noises made by Germany generated far less interest than those made by the eighteen sound-effects men specially recruited by the Palace's Vivian van Damm to bring the film noisily to life.

Working behind the screen, with rear-projection to help them follow the story, they banged twenty-three drums of varying sizes and sounds, fired off rifles, revolvers and magnesium flares, splashed around with a shower bath, which dripped on to stretched tarpaulin to make rain, and released an enormous cylinder of compressed air to create the snorting of the mythical beast of war. And the highlight of their action-packed routine came, twice-daily, when the Palace firemen gathered around a great tank in which maroons were let off electronically—producing, as one who saw it reported, 'noise, reeking smoke and general pandemonium, which made it appear like a visitation from the Four Horsemen themselves.'

Flash, bang, wallop. It was quite a picture.

THIRTEEN

But—Oh! ye lords of ladies intellectual
Inform us truly, have they not hen-pecked you all?
                George Gordon, Lord Byron (1788–1824)

NOW A DYNAMIC, domineering and, eventually, disastrous
figure crossed the path—or, rather, film set—of Rudolph
Valentino.

He first saw her as she walked across a setting for
Uncharted Seas, and he was instantly, utterly and irredeemably captivated.

First, he remembered later, he saw Alla Nazimova, the
'incomparable' Russian whose cheap gigolo jibe had
brought him to tears of anger and frustration. He eyed
her warily as she stopped to watch a rehearsal on his set.
Then he switched his eyes to the girl standing talking to
her, and could not take them away.

She was stunningly attractive, tall, graceful, and very,
very beautiful. Her oval face had strong, yet delicate,
almost aristocratic features. Her eyes were brown, mysterious, searching, and her dark auburn hair, long and
luxuriant, was coiled in braids that seemed to form, he
said, a halo. She looked, to Valentino, like some queen
from a storybook. Even that was too meagre and mediocre a description: 'I saw before me no ordinary woman,
but rather the reincarnation of some mighty goddess of
the past.'

She glanced, for an instant, his way. Her eyes, which

in seconds had him bewitched, swept over him as he stared at her, transfixed. Then, with Nazimova, she walked on and out of his sight.

'Who,' he asked a member of the film crew, 'was that?'

'Natacha,' he was told. 'Natacha Rambova. A friend of Nazimova's. Her set and costume designer.'

Within days, Valentino knew a great deal more than that: her real name was, in fact, Winifred Shaunessey De Wolfe Hudnut, and she was the stepdaughter of American cosmetics millionaire Richard Hudnut. She had been to school in England and decided on a career in dancing. She had studied with the Russian Ballet's Theodore Kosloff and, after touring America dancing as his partner, had met Nazimova. And now, with a new and much more impressive name, she was beginning a new career with the Russian star who had befriended her.

She was also, although Valentino could not know it yet, wilful, determined, headstrong and dedicated to the success of that career—a gorgeously beautiful woman whose dazzling smile hid her strong will and burning ambition to become a somebody in the film world and not merely 'the make-up magnate's stepdaughter'.

Valentino wanted desperately to know her, to love her. Yet she, it appeared, thought of him as nothing, far beneath her—a low, uncultured actor who had no place in the life of the rich, artistic and generously-gifted and talented girl that she, without any self-deprecatory doubts, knew herself to be.

Whenever he saw her, or tried to catch her eye and flash that previously always successful smile in her direction, she ignored him. Completely and absolutely. His Italian pride was deeply wounded, his confidence shaken,

Above With Carmel Myers in 'A Society Sensation' (1918).
Below With Dorothy Gish in 'Out of Luck' (1919).

As Julio in 'The Four Horsemen of the Apocalypse' (1920). *Opposite* With Nazimova in 'Camille' (1921).

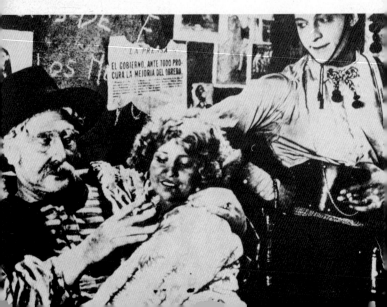

and the only way he could get to know her, he decided, was to somehow arrange a formal introduction.

No devious plots were necessary. The introduction, when it came, was through the last source he thought possible—from Nazimova herself, the woman who had ordered him from her table, the internationally-famous star who had established herself during the war years by appearing in a series of propaganda films.

Now, hoping to bolster her sagging reputation with a box-office winner, she planned to make *Camille*, and was looking for a dark, handsome and passionate type of actor to play the Frenchman Armand to her Marguerite. Valentino was the obvious choice from among the Metro men, and when she put the idea to him he was overjoyed. Not only because he would be playing opposite a big-name star, but because it would give him the opportunity to get to know, and to work closely with, the woman he could not (and never would) chase from his mind.

Nazimova introduced him to Natacha shortly afterwards when Rudolph, in heavy fur costume, walked off the set of *Uncharted Seas*. Nervously, he bowed low and looked into her eyes and smiled. The smile which she returned, to his overwhelming delight, was, some would say, one of immense satisfaction.

From that moment he was completely under her spell and control, and Natacha, realising that Nazimova's term of power in Hollywood had almost run its course, would use and dominate him in her all-consuming ambition to become a power herself. He would become her new patron, whom she would enslave with her body and dominate with her mind. Through her, he would lose many months of his fast-rising career. Because of her, friends would desert him, directors shun him and top studios say they didn't want to know him. She would bring him to realms of happiness that he did not believe existed, and depths of depression that he almost could not bear.

For the time being, she said simply: 'Pleased to meet you, Mr. Valentino.'

When shooting started on *Camille* (and for Valentino that could not be soon enough) it became immediately clear who was to be in charge. Although it was the first time Natacha Rambova had worked in a film studio, and she was technically responsible only for design, the fiercely-independent loner from Salt Lake City used her influence with Nazimova to dominate the production. She treated established film-makers as her inferiors, and even director Ray Smallwood dared not block her.

She paid special attention to Valentino, to his hair, his costume, his style. If hers was a blatantly unsubtle approach, the entranced Valentino was only too willing to go along with her plans for self-glorification. This girl, he was certain, was the one who would at last bring him the romantic happiness he had searched for in vain. She would be his wife, and the mother of the children he longed to have.

That this was no brief and passing affair soon became apparent to them both—and to most of the studio—with their widely-broadcast act of love on the day-bed of Valentino's dressing-room while his leading lady sat impatiently waiting on the set just yards away for him to resume his less-passionate, but equally romantic, role as a hero for the benefit of the world's moviegoers.

Their clothes, hastily thrown off in their urgency, lay on the thickly-carpeted floor as they expressed their love. Only the untimely interruption of the assistant, following Smallwood's order to find out what was delaying Valentino, marred those moments for Natacha and the man

98

destined to become the idol of millions. For him even the following scandal of the naked-topped 'beauty contest' line-up, and persistent stories of a 'harem', meant nothing. He had met the woman he was sure he had been destined for.

That certain knowledge was reinforced during the following weeks as he and Natacha discovered more about each other. They had, they found, much in common, despite the wide gulf in their backgrounds. Both knew, and loved, dancing and the film-world. Both were lonely and ambitious. And both would confront together the looming crisis in Valentino's career.

It came when Metro asked him to work with Alice Terry in *The Conquering Power*, which June Mathis had adapted from Balzac's *Eugenie Grandet*. Rex Ingram was the director and the *Four Horsemen* crew had been lined-up for the production. It looked like a winner, except that Valentino's attitude to his career seemed to have changed: he was much more self-assured, a little less eager-to-please and ready to do what was asked of him. And he wanted more money—a rise of one hundred dollars in his salary.

It was clear to more than a few that the influence of the ambitious Natacha was already at work, pressing him on to better things, urging him not to sell his talent for the first sum that was mentioned. There were rows at the studio and, grudgingly, Valentino eventually accepted a rise of fifty dollars, bringing his salary to four hundred dollars a week. But, still far from happy, he was at the centre of more squabbles on the set with Rex Ingram, who could not quite understand how the charming, helpful, conscientious actor of a few months ago had suddenly become a temperamental, arrogant and moody man.

The crew noticed that, too. 'Valentino,' one said, 'should know better than to fight with Ingram. Actors don't impress him—he makes actors. He may be exacting, but he's the best.'

The film dragged on in an atmosphere of almost-constant hostility and, when it was finally finished, it was difficult to know who was the happier—the star or the director. Certainly, Ingram was said to have threatened never to work with Valentino again, and Valentino felt much the same way. Despite the interventions of June Mathis as a 'peace-maker', their professional collaboration was at an end. Valentino decided to quit Metro. And to return for a while, to the wilderness.

*   *   *

For eight long, frustrating months, he would do nothing. And, because Nazimova had no immediate project on the stocks, Natacha would do nothing with him. They retreated together to a tiny cottage on Sunset Boulevard—so small that when Natacha's mother arrived one evening, she thought it was the garage and wondered where the actual *residence* could be.

For a time Rudolph was supremely content away from the squabbles and tensions of film-making and able to spend his time making Italian meals for, and love to, his 'goddess'. Even Natacha seemed comparatively happy. Looking back, she would call it 'the best time I could expect to live through'. They talked, and loved, and planned for the time they would be able to marry.

Rudolph wanted a real home, and a family, and Natacha wanted children, too. 'But we should wait,' she told him, her eye again on her career, 'until you are really established.'

They were wise words. As the weeks stretched into

100

months, and no work prospects appeared, the lavish-spending couple realised that they were broke. Even though her family were rich, Natacha maintained a determined independence and would not ask for money. Work, they were sure, would soon be offered to them. In the meantime, they were often so hard-up and hungry that they would go poaching rabbits together for their evening meal.

In time, though, the attractions of this hand-to-mouth, sex-and-spaghetti existence waned. They needed money, and money meant work. Natacha urged Valentino to visit the studios of Famous Players-Lasky (Paramount) and talk to the company's chief, Jesse L. Lasky, about the possibility of a film role. He was welcomed with interest, and some variation of the line 'Don't call us, we'll call you.'

But when they did call, it would be with something very big indeed.

FOURTEEN

The desert were a paradise
If thou wert there, if thou were there

Robert Burns (1759–96)

IN THE EVENING silence of her neat, well-ordered farm-house, Edith Maud Winstanley patted her greying hair into place, pushed the granny glasses firmly on to the bridge of her nose and, with just a little more application than other women brought to the composition of their shopping lists, continued to create a worldwide sensation.

The shy, retiring wife of a gentleman farmer sent her imagination soaring beyond the bleak Derbyshire countryside to the shimmering sands of Araby where, under the blazing desert sun, her beautiful and pale-complexioned heroine, Diana Mayo, had been captured by a brutal beast of a sheik who was to force her (although she didn't know it yet) into sexual submission again and again.

Diana's eyes passed over him slowly till they rested on his brown, clean-shaven face, surmounted by crisp, close-cut brown hair. It was the handsomest and the cruellest face that she had ever seen. Her gaze was drawn instinctively to his. He was looking at her with fierce burning eyes that swept her until she felt that the boyish clothes that covered her slender limbs were stripped from her, leaving her beautiful white body bare under his passionate stare. She shrank back, quivering, dragging the

102

lapels of her riding jacket together over her breast with clutching hands, obeying an impulse that she hardly understood. 'Who are you?' she gasped hoarsely.

'I am the Sheik Ahmed Ben Hassan . . .'

Edith's husband Percy, who bred prize pigs and preferred not to talk too much about his wife's romantic scribblings, might not like her writing like this. The neighbours would, no doubt, be more than shocked to learn that they lived not a rapist's leap from a woman who wrote such things. But the money for books was good—sometimes more than £50—and it helped eke out the family funds when times were hard. Edith would press on, no matter what they might say:

She looked, dry-eyed, she had no tears left. They had all been expended when she had grovelled at his feet, imploring the mercy he had not accorded her. She had fought until the unequal struggle had left her exhausted and helpless in his arms, until her whole body was one agonised ache from the brutal hands that forced her to compliance, until her courageous spirit was crushed by the realisation of her own powerlessness, and by the strange fear that the man himself awakened in her, which had driven her at last moaning to her knees.

People would, Edith knew as she wrote, call it sensationalism, sado-masochism, near-pornography. The very thought of a nice young English gel being ravished by some nasty little wog would appall and horrify them and they would call it 'trash' fit only for under-housemaids. Yet they would read it, because it took them far away from drab reality to the distant desert where romance was rough and ready and very, very, readable.

Stooping, he disengaged her clinging fingers from the heavy drapery and drew her hands slowly together up to his breast with a little smile. 'Come,' he whispered, his

103

passionate eyes devouring her. She fought against the fascination with which they dominated her, resisting him dumbly with tight-locked lips till he held her palpitating in his arms. 'Little fool,' he said with a deepening smile. 'Better me than my men.'

The gibe broke her silence. 'Oh, you brute! You brute!' she wailed, until his kisses silenced her.

Edith smiled to herself. Her public would be shocked to learn that E. M. Hull, the pen-name she thought it best to write under, was not some widely-experienced man-of-the-world, but a little farmer's wife from Derbyshire. But she knew, better than any man, what women wanted to read, and a happy ending was an essential ingredient of her secret.

The Sheik, she would reveal, was no nasty Arab at all, but the son of a true-blue English peer—the Earl of Glencaryll, no less—who'd been brought up (through no fault of his own) by the old sheik and had grown naturally into those disgusting, degrading, desert ways. And Diana would declare, on the last page, that she was deeply and desperately in love with the chap.

The colour stole back slowly into her face and a little tremulous smile curved her lips. She slid her arm up and round his neck, drawing his head down. 'I am not afraid,' she murmured slowly. 'I am not afraid of anything with your arms around me, my desert lover. Ahmed! Monseigneur.'

As she wrote the last lines, Edith Maud Winstanley was fairly certain she had a success on her hands. Although even her wild imagination could not let her foresee just how massively successful it would be and what a shattering effect her work would have on the world's standards and styles and fashions. And, especially, on the life of Rudolph Valentino.

It hit the public like a hard, unexpected, slap in the face from a threatened, enraged woman. *The Sheik* (first published in Britain by Eveleigh Nash and Grayson in 1919, and later in America) was a runaway success. Some critics called it tosh. The public called it great and sat there, thumbing through its pages and panting for more as the wretched Diana Mayo suffered unspeakable torment at the hands of that beast.

It was read in tens of thousands of respectable homes, both upstairs and downstairs, by the servants and the served, the wealthy and the waiters-on, and they all loved every last ravishing word of it. Especially those last ravishing words.

Its success was repeated in America, and among those who devoured it at very few readings was a member of Jesse Lasky's staff, who urged him to make a film of the book. Convinced by her rave recommendation, Lasky wondered who could play the leading male role and, happily, remembered Valentino's call.

He returned the call, offered Valentino a salary of five hundred dollars a week to play the Sheik, and the now-impecunious Rudolph leapt at the chance. To him, after months below the breadline, it was a marvellous, heaven-sent, opportunity. But to Natacha it was merely a chance to appear in what would obviously be a cheap and nasty movie. 'The story is trash,' she told him. 'You can't do it. It will ruin whatever reputation you already have.'

Valentino, disappointed that she was not as excited as him about the offer, tried to argue its merits. He failed miserably. 'You will never become a true artist if you accept the first thing that comes along,' Natacha protested. 'And this is no good for you.'

She was, of course, wildly wrong, but Natacha Rambova was never one to be moved by rational argument.

As an excited and enthusiastic Rudolph prepared to make the film, which he was certain would give him a dynamic and rugged new image, she constantly scoffed at the role, the script, the plot. It would do his image harm, she said. He would be laughed out of the cinemas.

In that, some critics were inclined to agree with her. When the film was released, the reviews were cool. Valentino and Agnes Ayres, according to the general consensus of critical opinion, did well in what was an unrealistic, wildly romantic saga set in the sand. Pure hokum. But if Natacha was about to say 'I told you so,' she would be speaking too soon: the public, as they had with Edith Hull's book, ignored the critics and made up their own minds. And in their minds there were absolutely no doubts whatsoever. This was It!

This was Romance and Excitement and Passion and Adventure. This was Love and Lust and Sex and Savagery served up just the way they loved it. And here, at last, was a virile, dominant and demanding hero—a man who knew what he wanted and made sure he got it. When Valentino moved those large, almost occult eyes until vast areas of white were visible, drew back the lips of his wide, sensuous mouth to bare gleaming teeth, flared his nostrils and ordered the captive Agnes Ayres 'Lie still, you little fool!' women trembled and whimpered and sighed and simmered to the point of ecstasy. He demanded their attention and they gave it, willingly, lovingly, longingly.

Even men, openly professing contempt for a boyish-faced hero who lounged around the desert smoking scented cigarettes, had to admit that he had a certain style; that he could swash a nifty buckle. Coming clean, Damon Runyan admitted: 'He made me long for a fleet steed in the Sahara and the licence to capture any swell-looking Judys I found running around loose on the desert.'

But Valentino, doubtless after consultations with Natacha, decided the whole thing was nonsense. '*The Sheik*,' he said, 'was my idea of a poor performance. I hate it.' Asked why, he pointed out that the sheik was an Arab-Englishman. No Arab or Englishman goes in for the display of emotion. 'So why,' he asked of his questioners, 'all that eye-rolling?'

It was too late now for damn-fool questions like that. The Sheik bandwagon was beginning to rattle and roll. In all, some 125,000,000 were to see the film. Sheik fashions were to become the rage, for women and men. Vaseline, and other hair-care applications, would experience a significant sales-boost. A song called *The Sheik of Araby* would be on everyone's lips. There would be a spate of follow-up films and shows. And men (and women) would take to seriously reconsidering the techniques of courtship and love-making.

Even the English language would not be immune from the onslaught: from now, dictionary definitions of sheik(h) would not be merely 'Chief, head of Arabian or Mohammedan tribe, family, or village', but also 'masterful husband or lover, dashing or attractive man'.

Eminent psychiatrists and noted psychologists and other assorted mental specialists would try to analyse and explain this curious social phenomenon with learned phrases like 'emotional vulnerability', 'sexual immaturity', 'public hysteria' and 'lack of inhibitory checks'. But to impressionable young girls and experienced mature women alike, as they sat in darkened cinemas transfixed by that flickering image on the screen, the secret was much more obvious.

It was the magic of that dark, dashing, desert devil,

The Great Lover, the screen's first he-man sex symbol.
It was all down to that one magnificent, marvellous man.
And to one woman.

In her neat, well-ordered farmhouse, Edith Maud
Winstanley read the latest item about the new star called
Valentino and then put the newspaper aside. There was a
lot of work ahead of her: *Shadow of the East* (1921), *The
Desert Healer* (1922), *Sons of the Sheik* (1922), *Camp-
ing in the Sahara* (1926), *The Lion Tamer* (1927)...

Edith, a woman who knew what the world wanted,
smiled to herself and sent her vivid imagination soaring,
once again, beyond the bleak Derbyshire landscape outside...

FIFTEEN

Marriage is nothing but a civil contract.
John Selden (1584–1654)

ON NOVEMBER 23, 1921—just a little over two years after their tragi-comic wedding—Rudolph Valentino and Jean Acker faced each other across a Los Angeles courtroom before Judge Thomas Toland. Each sought a divorce from the other, and their evidence was expected to clash on almost every headline-making point. The Hollywood gossips and journalists were not to be disappointed.

Giving evidence first, Jean Acker claimed that two months after marrying her Valentino had entered her apartment, invaded the bathroom while she was naked in the bath and hit her. Then he told her he did not wish to stay married to her and asked her to help fabricate the divorce evidence.

Appearing sick and miserable, she sat in the witness box and in a faint voice explained that she had started work as an actress at the age of eighteen and by the time she filed her suit for maintenance had been earning up to two hundred dollars a week.

When a man married, she declared, she thought he was in a position to take care of his wife. She had not known Valentino was so broke. To have had him in her hotel would have embarrassed her. She had given him money, clothes and underwear and wanted him to go to work.

Asked why she had not allowed Valentino to visit her while she was filming on location Jean told the court, amid laughter, that there were only two single beds in her hotel room—and a girlfriend had been visiting her. She agreed that the only real support she had given her husband was that he used too much of her perfume.

Metro executive Maxwell Karger and his wife said in evidence that Jean Acker had told how sorry she was that she and Valentino had married.

She had remarked to Karger that she thought it best if they separate.

Taking the witness stand, highly nervous and with a distinct stammer, Valentino told of his confusion on the night of his wedding. How he had pleaded with his wife to admit him to the bedroom. There had been no question of his forcing her to marry him and he was completely unable to explain her behaviour. He had, he said, believed Jean Acker to be a normal woman.

He did admit striking her, under extreme provocation, when she insulted him after agreeing to meet him and discuss a reconciliation.

'I took her to be my wife for better or worse, whether I be rich or whether I be poor,' he said. He had loved her and always hoped that she would agree to live with him.

When Jean took the stand again, she finally admitted to the packed courtroom that the marriage had never been consummated. She had spent one night with her husband in his apartment, a month after their wedding. But they did not make love.

On January 10 Judge Toland announced his decision: there was desertion on the part of Jean Acker, and Rudolph Valentino was entitled to a divorce on that ground.

Jean left the court in tears, the sympathetic arm of a

close woman friend around her waist. Valentino exuberantly hugged his attorney, friends and reporters and, with the assistance of a local Speakeasy owner, invited them to celebrate his victory in illicit champagne. That evening, during dinner with Natacha, Valentino's happiness was lifted to new heights when she accepted his proposal of marriage.

But Natacha, ironically in view of the scandal and legal quagmire into which they were soon to become entangled, insisted that before they could marry he must rid himself entirely of the problem of Jean Acker.

The Judge had made no order regarding maintenance. Valentino, she insisted, must arrange through his attorney to make a once-and-for-all payment to his former wife. He agreed, and in May was able to sign legal papers with Jean Acker contracting to pay her 12,100 dollars, in return for which she promised to release him from all future claims for alimony and legal fees.

Paramount loaned him 5,000 dollars to pay the first instalment and he agreed to pay the balance at fixed intervals.

With his head out of one matrimonial noose, Rudolph Valentino felt he could begin to breathe more easily, unaware that the strangling threads of another were already insinuating themselves, garrotte-like, about his throat.

SIXTEEN

Love is the wisdom of the fool
And the folly of the wise.

Dr. Samuel Johnson (1709–84)

DURING THE PREPARATION for his court appearance and
the divorce hearing, the all-important question of Valentino's future film career had also to be answered.

Friends like director Douglas Gerrard, Norman Kerry
and Bob Florey urged him to take Paramount's advice
and, unless the studio appeared to be deliberately down-
grading him with their choice of pictures, stick to the
schedule they laid down for him.

Natacha, on the other hand, believed that only she
could successfully and meaningfully guide her lover's
advancement in Hollywood. Certainly, she agreed, *The
Sheik* had brought him enormous popularity—a thousand letters a week were flooding in to Paramount's publicity office—but he now owed it to himself, and to her,
to take only the kind of artistic roles which would win
him the critical acclaim he deserved.

Valentino reminded her that she had dismissed *The
Sheik* as rubbish, pure and unmitigated, and predicted
that it would finish his career. Far from that, he pointed
out, it had established him as a superstar and lifted his
salary to a level that was almost keeping pace with their
spending.

Even so, he was apprehensive as he approached her

bungalow on Sunset Boulevard after agreeing with Paramount vice-president Jesse Lasky to appear in *Moran of the Lady Letty*, based on the Frank Norris novel.

Natacha's reaction was just as explosive as he had feared. For almost an hour she berated him, cursing his gutter-level taste and lack of manliness in not facing up to Lasky.

'He is making a fool of you!' she screamed. 'How can you inject art into this putrid garbage?'

Valentino drew himself up to his full five feet, eleven inches and pulled out what he believed to be the winning trick to their argument. 'He also raised my salary to seven hundred a week—without my even asking,' he announced.

'Fool!' yelled Natacha, with renewed fury. 'He would have given you a thousand if you'd asked for it. If you've agreed, I suppose you will have to go through with it ... and I'll have to make it as unshoddy as possible.'

Valentino's bewildering eagerness to accept her advice on all aspects of film-making exasperated his friends and tried the patience of director George Melford who, after his triumph with *The Sheik*, had been assigned to the Italian's new picture.

Though his criticisms lacked enthusiasm and obviously did not originate in his own head, Valentino questioned the interior designs, costumes and camera angles and brought the lighting team almost to the point of strike action.

This preoccupation with artistry was all very well, said Melford, but audiences were paying to see Valentino in action, not to admire his clothes and the sets. This realistic piece of advice from the director had no outward effect on his star actor but, to the intense relief of everyone associated with the picture, *Moran of the Lady Letty* was completed without a major studio row.

Meanwhile, *The Sheik* continued to break all box office records and Paramount, determined to keep their petulant young star happy, offered to raise his salary to 1,250 dollars a week and cast him opposite Gloria Swanson in the screen version of Elinor Glyn's novel *Beyond the Rocks*, which they had recently bought. Elinor Glyn, whose chief claim to fame had been coining the word 'It' for sex appeal, was an English writer whose work tended to concentrate on her own passionate support of more emancipation for women.

Beyond the Rocks had been panned by the literary critics and its theme dismissed as depraved and unsavoury, and Valentino's agreement to appear in the screen version provoked yet another contemptuous and vituperative harangue from Natacha. If his ambition was to ruin his career before it became firmly established, she said, then starring in this trashy society drama was one of the quickest ways to achieve it.

The news that Gloria Swanson, one of the most famous of the original Mack Sennett Bathing Beauties, was to co-star with Rudy slightly mollified his outraged fiancée—but she informed him that the only possible way he could contemplate going through with this 'insult to his talents' was by insisting on her full-time presence on the set.

The addition of his friend Gertrude Astor to the cast helped to ease tension for Valentino, who found himself under constant crossfire from Natacha and the man on the megaphone, Sam Wood. Quite naturally, Wood had believed he would have full control of the picture when Jesse Lasky invited him to direct. He knew Natacha by reputation, but no-one had warned him about her temper, her determination and her almost hypnotic control of the man recently acclaimed the world's greatest screen lover.

Valentino used the pressure of fan mail to escape most of their highly defamatory and roasting exchanges, but when roped in by his fuming mistress, he invariably sided with her against the unfortunate director. Paramount had by this time assigned two secretaries to him to cope with his correspondence, and he kept them just off the set, ostentatiously dictating to them during every break from shooting. Natacha's presence also did little to smooth the somewhat cool relationship that developed after the first few days between Valentino and Gloria Swanson. There were no hostile scenes, but it was clear to the whole cast and crew that the two stars were hardly enamoured of one another.

Valentino's habit of taking on the character of the part he was playing was partly to blame for the tense situation: in *The Four Horsemen*, while playing Julio, he became pleasant, philosophical and sensitive; As Lord Bracondale in *Beyond the Rocks*, he became indecisive, superior and jealous, criticising the script and the plot and protesting that some of the best scenes were going to lesser players.

Once again Jesse Lasky was besieged by angry and frustrated technicians, from the director down, complaining about the non-cooperation and hypercriticism of Valentino and the wilful arrogance of the female Svengali who manipulated him. Lasky pleaded for patience and understanding. The divorce hearing had placed a considerable strain on the Italian, he said. It was a difficult time for all of them, but the picture was what counted. The studio's newest fulgent personality was cursed and despised by the crew, but Lasky's appeal prevented open disruption of the schedule and *Beyond the Rocks* was finished on time.

Valentino's victory in the divorce court had restored his customary Latin ebullience, and even Natacha was elated when Lasky summoned his star to the studios and revealed that he was to feature in another Ibanez adaptation, *Blood and Sand*.

He broke down and wept in the Vice-President's office. But they were tears of joy. The part of Juan Gallardo was one he wanted more than any other.

Not since *The Sheik* had he considered a role so perfectly suited to his particular talents. 'This will be the greatest performance of my career,' he promised. It was the kind of exotic costume role in which he excelled, and Lasky's additional news that his friend George Fitzmaurice was to direct the picture lifted Valentino to new peaks of happiness.

Excitedly he told Natacha that as the film was to be shot on location in Spain, he planned to precede the crew there to take special instruction in bullfighting and so bring added authenticity to his portrayal of Ibanez's matador hero.

Therefore an announcement from Paramount that Fitzmaurice was not available to film *Blood and Sand*, and that it had been decided to shoot the picture in Hollywood rather than Spain, provoked such a monumental rage in Valentino that Lasky fled the studios and refused to meet him until staff assured him that Rudy's temper had subsided. He agreed to see him only after Valentino was told that Paramount had obtained the services of Fred Niblo, considered universally within the profession to be one of the top directors in Hollywood.

This sop to his ego somewhat appeased Valentino, but once face-to-face with Lasky he complained bitterly about the switch of locations. To achieve the authentic atmosphere it needed to be filmed in Spain, he said. Sensing the voice of Natacha behind Valentino's protestations, Lasky swore that the sets in Hollywood would be exact reproductions of actual Spanish constructions, faithfully copied down to the last dab of cement.

But what about his instruction in the art of bullfighting? snapped the star, finally breaching the subject about which he felt most strongly. He would require the exclusive services of a top matador, who must be on hand throughout production.

Happy to concede this small point, after having overcome Valentino's major complaints, Lasky promised that such a man would be found. A fortnight later Rudolph had the services of a new dresser, an ex-matador who, for the exorbitant fees demanded for him by the actor, was delighted to school him in all the traditional and flamboyant arts of bullfighting.

Valentino even won a concession from Lasky to be allowed to practise his newly-acquired skills in a portable bull ring—although he was limited to facing only young bulls or horned cows, and an armed guard stood by to intervene if the valuable human property found himself in difficulties.

Despite his childish delight in strutting the sands of his personal arena, Valentino was far from ready to capitulate to all the studio's other demands. Taking upon himself many of the arrogant characteristics of Juan Gallardo, and more than adequately primed by Natacha, he treated the film personnel and director Niblo with calculated contempt. At the slightest sign of opposition he would storm off the set, and work on the picture was painfully slow.

To his great surprise, he discovered that his bigbreasted co-star Nita Naldi was firmly on his side and more than willing to support him in his frequent clashes with authority.

Even the choice of dressing room allocated to him turned into a slanging match between Valentino and Lasky's minions. Knowing perfectly well that a dressing room with private bathroom was unavailable, Rudolph nevertheless demanded this as his right. Filming ceased for a whole day, and in the end Lasky had to intervene to get the cameras turning again.

Natacha, whose experience of film-making was negligible compared to that of Niblo, insisted on being present at all times, and in her aggressively self-opinionated way challenged the famous director on virtually every pronouncement he made.

Knowing that his star would perform more willingly when Natacha was there to support him, Lasky argued in favour of her continued presence. But Fred Niblo, resenting the flagrant manner in which she was presuming on his role, finally delivered an ultimatum: If Natacha wasn't taken off the set, he would quit.

Valentino retorted that if Natacha was barred from the studio he would consider himself barred, too. Almost at his wits' end, and complaining to anyone who would listen that never before had a studio executive been plagued by such an intolerable, pretentious and overbearing pair, Lasky called in the warring trio and managed to negotiate an uneasy truce.

Incredibly, despite all the tantrums and stoppages— but in good part because of Niblo's patience and genius—Valentino fulfilled the promise he made to Lasky at the outset and turned in one of the finest performances of his career.

Viewing the first rough cut of the picture, Lasky forgot about the feuds, ordered an even larger team of Paramount publicity men into action to further swell the Valentino legend, and took his recalcitrant star and his fiancée out on the town to celebrate.

Paramount had another multi-million box office block-buster on their hands. Valentino, the man who had saved Metro, would single-handedly establish the newly-formed Paramount as one of the giants of the film industry. Already envisioning the fortunes to come, Lasky declared himself delighted when the happy couple told him they planned to marry.

The Vice-President, like them, was not fully familiar with the vagaries of Californian law. And was therefore unaware that he had toasted a proposal which could terminate his money-making star's Hollywood career, and was destined to land him in jail as key figure in a major scandal.

SEVENTEEN

There was an old party of Lyme,
Who married three wives at one time,
When asked, 'Why the third?'
He replied 'One's absurd,
And bigamy, sir, is a crime!'

Cosmo Monkhouse (1840–1901)

FOR HOLLYWOOD AND for Rudolph Valentino 1922 was a bad year.

It was the year that filmland's capital earned itself the title of Sin City and the Olympians of the dream-making industry were exposed as mere mortals with very basic weaknesses of the flesh. Rape, orgies, murder, perversion and drug-taking provided running scandals that kept the tabloids in a frenzy of lurid disclosures which were to tarnish the image of the Golden People for a decade.

The first paroxysmal event was the arrest of popular comedian Roscoe 'Fatty' Arbuckle for the rape and murder of startlet Virginia Rappe. Eventually he was charged with manslaughter and aquitted—but his career was irredeemably wrecked.

Then came the murder, never solved, of Paramount's leading director, English-born William Desmond Taylor. It was an outrageous and depraved business involving drugs, sexual perversion and an unofficial harem of Hollywood starlets. Taylor, it transpired, was the main practitioner of the 'casting couch' technique, a notorious profligate who collected items of underwear from his starry-eyed conquests and filed them, labelled with names and dates, in a special chamber in his home.

To add to the juiciness of the scandal, it was revealed that two of the lustful director's mistresses—affairs pursued at one and the same time—were movie heroines Mabel Normand, a Mack Sennett star, and Mary Miles Minter. It was even suggested that Minter's own mother had succumbed to Taylor's lewd approaches.

Shocked but fascinated film fans had barely taken in these sordid disclosures when it was announced that matinee idol Wallace Reid had died in an asylum while undergoing treatment to cure his drug addition.

Hollywood moguls, anxious to correct this degenerate image, and fearful that public reaction would manifest itself in a box office boycott, approached a member of President Harding's Cabinet, Postmaster-General Will H. Hays, and invited him to become their 'czar', with far-reaching powers to stamp out any evils in motion pictures or, currently more important, among those who made them.

In May 1922, Hays arrived in Los Angeles and was greeted by Jesse Lasky and United Artists President Joseph Schenck. The thin, abstemious midwesterner announced that his first task would be to probe the off-screen conduct of the stars and force them to meet the high standards of respectability he intended to introduce as a matter of extreme urgency.

Lasky, whose company distributed Arbuckle's movies, and had Taylor under contract at the time of his murder, squirmed uncomfortably as Hays recounted the disturbing effect on public morals that these squalid affairs were having—and then volunteered his full co-operation in stamping out immoral practices in the film capital.

But this spontaneous offer was to cause him untold anguish just a week later, when Hollywood's latest scandal swept all other items from the nation's front pages: Rudolph Valentino, the first honest-to-goodness sex symbol of the screen, and with a following of millions of impressionable female fans, had committed bigamy.

A phone call from Will Hays followed the newspapers into Lasky's office within minutes. To prevent accusations that the industry condoned this kind of blatant immorality, he told the agitated studio boss, it might prove necessary to blacklist Valentino.

As Lasky clapped his palms to his forehead in despair, a hundred miles away in Palm Springs the newlyweds were having their first doubts about the wisdom of their romantic gesture.

Both had been aware that the divorce from Jean Acker would not become final until the following year, but Valentino was convinced that if they married in Mexico they could not be charged with violating Californian law. Airily he explained that other impatient couples, some in the film business, had married in Mexico or in another state without legal repercussions.

He ignored or chose to overlook the fact that those others had been protected by a certain degree of anonymity. But when he and Natacha drove across the Mexican border on May 13, with Douglas Gerrard and another friend, Paul Ivano, they were spotted within minutes of arriving in the small town of Mexicali.

By the time the mayor had been consulted, and agreed to perform the marriage ceremony, several thousand inhabitants had gathered around the old, stone-built town hall. While the mayor's deputy hurriedly gathered together the Mexicali military band, his wife recruited half a dozen other women, wives of the town's most prominent citizens, and began planning the special wedding feast her husband had decreed necessary to mark this signal honour being accorded his community.

Valentino and Natacha, who had planned a brief and preferably quiet wedding, were nevertheless flattered by this spontaneous gesture of goodwill, and the bridegroom agreed to make a speech to the several hundred people who turned up.

That evening the mayor and several carloads of cheering, exuberant admirers of the Hollywood newlyweds accompanied them to the border, and bid them an emotional farewell. From the border the couple drove north to Palm Springs to begin their honeymoon, which they planned to spend in the desert resort and in San Diego.

But two days later the newspaper headlines shocked them out of their euphoria. Reporters, wise in the ways of the Los Angeles courts, and sensing a far better story than the simple announcement that Valentino had married, checked with judges and court officials whose opinions were unanimous: the wedding in Mexicali had been a bigamous one.

Valentino's first impulse was to flee and put as much distance as possible between himself and the Californian officers of justice. Arrangements to depart that day for New York were well in hand when an anguished Jesse Lasky came on the telephone. Running away could only make matters worse, he yelled. The legal position was bad enough, but the opinion of Will Hays and the question of Valentino's film future was of paramount importance. If the lovesick star could bluff it out and return to Hollywood immediately, advised Lasky, Hays might be convinced that no serious case of immorality was involved.

'As far as you were concerned, you had been granted a

divorce,' Lasky bellowed down the phone. 'You didn't understand the part about the interlocutory decree.'

'He is right,' Valentino told Natacha. 'After all, I am supposed to be the great lover. The public might understand that I was blinded to these minor legal details by my love for you. We must go back to Los Angeles immediately. My public will forgive me.'

In the almost bare rooms of a house on Whitley Heights, Hollywood, which the Valentinos had bought and intended to furnish after their honeymoon, they held a council of war with Lasky, studio lawyers and Rudolph's own attorney, Mr. W. I. Gilbert. All agreed that the less the couple were seen in each other's company the better, until the whole sorry mess had been sorted out, and it was decided that Natacha should leave for New York that very afternoon.

On the Sunday morning of May 21, at the request of the District Attorney—who had already publicly stated his intention to prosecute for bigamy—Valentino went to the Los Angeles municipal offices and entered a plea of guilty before a Justice of the Peace. Bail was granted on production of a surety of ten thousand dollars.

But it was a Sunday, pointed out Valentino's attorney. To find that amount of cash quickly would be difficult, although he could promise it would be produced the following morning. In that case, so would the defendant, snapped the D.A., and ordered Valentino to the cells.

Thrown in among the normal weekend bag of drunks, pimps and petty thieves, he screamed non-stop abuse at his jailors who had, as laid down in police regulations, emptied his pockets and removed his tie, braces and laces before putting him behind bars.

That Paramount did not have ten thousand dollars in cash, even on a Sunday, appeared inconceivable to the outraged actor. He believed, almost certainly correctly, that the studio were deliberately holding back to teach him a lesson, and swore that when extricated from this position of injust persecution, he would teach Paramount and Jesse Lasky a lesson.

Meanwhile Douglas Gerrard, who had been a witness at the wedding, was one of the few people actively seeking a solution to Rudy's predicament. He contacted a close friend, San Francisco Chief of Police Dan O'Brian, who was visiting Los Angeles, and explained about the exorbitant bail fixed for Valentino's release.

O'Brian sympathised but said he was unable to raise that kind of money on a Sunday. By chance, actor Thomas Meighan was with the police chief and overheard the telephone conversation.

Unaware of the identity of the person in trouble, but with the generosity for which he was famed, Meighan interrupted O'Brian and told him: 'If this friend of yours is in a jam, how much does he need?'

'Ten thousand bucks,' said O'Brian. 'Have you got it?'

'No, but I can get it soon enough,' replied Meighan. 'Who is it needs the dough?'

'Rudolph Valentino,' said the Police Chief. 'Still want to put the money up?'

'Yeah,' said Tommy Meighan, 'I think he's all right,' and hurried from the hotel, returning half an hour later with a certified cheque for ten thousand dollars. How he had managed to obtain the cheque O'Brian did not ask, but called Douglas Gerrard and told him he now had the means of getting Valentino out of jail.

By this time news of Rudy's imprisonment had swept through Los Angeles and a small army of reporters and photographers, together with several hundred fans, gathered outside the police headquarters. His attorney advised keeping to a brief, prepared statement, in which Valentino admitted he may have erred—but only because of his deep love for Natacha. To the American people, who had called him the greatest lover of the screen, he wished to say that the love responsible for his actions was prompted by the noblest intention that a man could have.

With only ten days to prepare their case—and instructed by Lasky that on no account must the hearing be allowed to drag out, or adjourned to a later date and thus preserved in the public eye—lawyers for Paramount and Valentino's personal attorney advised that his only hope of being cleared of the charge was to plead non-consummation of the marriage.

Rudy, who only four months before had used non-consummation as grounds for his divorce, wailed that his pride as a man could not let him submit to this kind of public humiliation again. Did they want the whole world to believe that he never went to bed with his women? he demanded. Patiently the lawyers explained that the only alternative to their suggestion was to accept the very real danger of a prison sentence. The bigamy case against him would be the first of its kind in California with international overtones. The State sentence for bigamy was from one to five years, and with this much publicity surrounding the case, no judge could do less than impose the minimum jail sentence. That was the best they could hope for.

Deeply embarrassed, Valentino acquiesced.

At the June hearing he sat beside his lawyers, unsmiling and for the most part head bowed, as seven witnesses who had been around during his alleged honeymoon in Palm Springs swore that he had never spent a single moment alone with Natacha after signing the marriage register in Mexicali. A court packed with schoolgirls, matrons and outrageously dressed flappers, stared fixedly at the star as they heard how he had never occupied the second single bed in his wife's room.

Natacha, it was stated, had been taken ill after their return from Mexico and a doctor had advised that she should sleep alone. Despite highly sarcastic questioning from the Deputy District Attorney, the witnesses maintained that Valentino had slept in a room with two men on the first night, and on a couch on the porch on the second night, of their stay in Palm Springs. The marriage had not been consummated, said his attorney, and thus could not be considered to have taken place.

The Judge agreed. On June 5 he announced that there was insufficient evidence to support the complaint. He felt that evidence of cohabitation could not be sufficiently shown to bring in a verdict of guilty from a jury. To save the county the great expense of a trial, he had decided to clear Valentino of the charge of bigamy.

Grudgingly, Rudy agreed with Lasky that the advice from studio attorneys had been well-founded and reluctantly accepted their further advice—that for the time being Natacha should keep away from Hollywood. The judge's ruling had cleared Valentino of immediate threat, but the District Attorney could still ask for Grand Jury action.

Even so, said Lasky smoothly, in terms of publicity the court hearing had been worth a million dollars, and it was planned to start work on his next picture immediately. Once again, Valentino agreed—but this accord with his employer was short-lived.

Rudolph wished to make *The Young Rajah*, scripted by June Mathis—a work that Lasky considered trite and lacking in any kind of entertainment value. He proposed several alternative subjects, but Valentino was intractable. Either Lasky would agree to *The Young Rajah* or he could cancel the company's contract with him.

Lasky capitulated. At least he did not have Natacha Rambova to contend with, he reassured himself. But he was mistaken. In voluntary exile from Hollywood, Natacha was quite determined not to resign her control of her 'almost' husband. To the utter despair of director Philip Rosen, Valentino telephoned her daily and did his utmost to follow her advice, which was generally contradictory to that handed out by the man on the megaphone. Each morning he appeared at the studio clutching copious notes and sketches forwarded to Los Angeles from the Adirondacks home of Natacha's stepfather and mother.

Valentino insisted that Natacha's designs and script changes be incorporated into the picture, even though some of the costume designs were so outlandish that Lasky, called in as an arbiter, completely lost control of himself and collapsed into a chair with tears of laughter rolling down his cheeks. Icily, Valentino waited until the paroxysm was over and then reiterated his decision to use the costume designs. Lasky replied that if he wished to deck himself in baubles, bangles and beads and make a public laughing stock of himself, he could go ahead. As long as the damned picture was finished quickly he could appear in skirts if he wished. Huffily Valentino retorted that Paramount and artistry were poles apart. He found it degrading to work for a company so reluctant to recognise the fruits of real artistic genius—for this was what he considered Natacha to be.

It was Lasky's turn to get angry. The studio had stood by Valentino throughout all his difficulties, he said. They had made him a star and, incidentally, advanced him

With Nita Naldi in 'Blood and Sand' (1922).

Valentino played a bullfighter in 'Blood and Sand'.

'The Young Rajah' (1922).

'Monsieur Beaucaire' (1922).

With Nita Naldi in 'A Sainted Devil' (1924).

'The Eagle' (1925) with Vilma Banky.

With Vilma Banky again in 'The Son of the Sheik' (1926).

A Christ-like Valentino dressed for 'The Hooded Falcon'. The film was never shot.

Valentino's most famous role was 'The Sheik' (1921) with Agnes Ayres; the story of an English girl ravished by an Arab in the burning desert. In the end they fall in love (*overleaf*).

With Gloria Swanson in 'Beyond the Rocks' (1922).

Close-up from 'Beyond the Rocks'.

more than 50,000 dollars over and above his salary to settle his first wife's maintenance and make the first payment on the Whitley Heights house. Perhaps it was Valentino's turn to do something for the studio in return? There was no conspiracy against him or Natacha, but Paramount were in the business of making pictures, not flattering egos. And pictures which, in future, would be chosen by the studio and not by the actor.

Seething, Valentino returned to the set, where he savagely criticised the long-suffering director's every observation—a tactic he maintained until the final scenes on *The Young Rajah* had been shot. Then, primed by Natacha, he again confronted Lasky and announced he would not be attending the Los Angeles or New York premieres of *Blood and Sand*. He had no intention of suffering the indignity of having his clothes torn off him by hysterical women of low intelligence.

Resolutely he defined his conditions for remaining with Paramount, the chief of which was the right to approve all scripts for his future films. If the studio denied him this right, he would consider them in breach of contract and take his services elsewhere.

The following morning he boarded the Eastbound train and headed directly for Foxlair Camp, the Hudnuts' home in the Adirondacks, and a reunion with Natacha. On September 2, in New York he read out a statement, which she had helped him prepare, which revealed that he was dissatisfied with Paramount and intended to leave the studio. Seemingly oblivious to the fact that Natacha's advice invariably landed him in trouble, Valentino had again acted on her counsel, without taking expert opinion.

Two weeks later Paramount retaliated to his 'I quit' statement with an injunction restraining him from entering into any contract with any other film production company. In December the Appellate Division in New York heard evidence from both sides. An attempt by Paramount to patch up their differences with the star, with an offer of 7,000 dollars a week and the right to consultation over the choice of films and director, had failed.

Natacha had refused to accept anything but total capitulation on the part of the studio. 'We will not even consider it,' she told Valentino. Secretly he believed the studio's offer to be an exceptionally generous one, particularly as once again he was being besieged by creditors, and his financial resources were totally non-existent. But, fearing to show any sign of weakness before his strong-willed 'wife', he agreed with her decision and told Paramount there could be no deal.

Paramount, in a prepared brief, listed many of Valentino's more hysterical demands and stressed his temperamental nature. Regrettably, reviews of *The Young Rajah* were poor and the film was doing only modest business compared with *Blood and Sand* and *The Sheik*. This, pointed out Lasky's lawyers, provided excellent proof of what happened when an actor was allowed to choose his own films. In this case Valentino's judgment had been utterly wrong. The studio was right in wanting to keep full control.

Valentino countered with accusations of insufficient and improper billing and poor dressing room facilities. He had been shadowed by detectives, he claimed, and Paramount had been cruel and insulting to Natacha, who was his wife in spirit, if not in fact.

The court was sympathetic but could not rule in Valentino's favour. He must either agree to work for Lasky at Paramount or retire from the film business until February, 1924—the date when his contract was due to end.

At a New York Press conference, Natacha answered for them both:

'Most of the films being selected today are an insult to the public's intelligence,' she said. 'If we are not to be allowed to alter this state of affairs by selecting our own pictures, then Mr. Valentino is better off removing himself from this artistic desert. He must at least be allowed to share artistic control with a director he trusts.'

Rudy stood grimly by, nodding his head sadly. In answer to further questions, he said he intended to write his biography and then embark on a visit to Europe, during which he would return to his birthplace and spend time with his brother and sister—although he did not explain where the money to finance the foreign jaunt was coming from.

News that Jean Acker was petitioning the courts to have her name changed from Jean Guglielmi to Jean Acker Valentino did not bring any comfort. Rudy wearily instructed his lawyers to file an objection. They accepted the brief and tactfully pointed out that, unless legal fees of more than 40,000 dollars could be paid quickly, their client might find himself involved in another court action—with themselves on the opposing side.

EIGHTEEN

I will be correspondent to command,
And do my spiriting gently.

William Shakespeare (1564–1616)

IT WAS DURING his court battles with Paramount that Valentino first became involved in spiritualism.

Natacha had been fascinated in the occult since her teens and frequently attended seances, but Rudy dismissed her beliefs as fantasies—until he witnessed a series of strange happenings at the West Sixty-seventh Street apartment that Natacha and her aunt, Mrs. Theresa Werner, had taken to be near his rooms in the Hotel des Artistes.

The 'happenings'—mysterious tapping in various parts of the apartment—were psychic attempts to establish contact, said Natacha—and they became more frequent whenever a friend of hers was paying a visit. The friend's mother was dying, and she believed the spirit messages concerned her ill health. The tapping reached a crescendo on the night the woman died. And then abruptly stopped.

A few weeks later the friend contacted Natacha and begged her and Rudolph to go with her to the home of a New York medium who, she said, had been receiving messages from the dead woman—and from Valentino's mother. Excited, somewhat scared and with, on Valentino's part, a degree of mistrust, they accompanied

Natacha's friend to the medium's apartment.

When they arrived, Valentino was handed a sheet of paper which drove out all his suspicions, and left him shaken and impressed. The paper contained, he believed, a message from his dead mother and mentioned details of his childhood unknown to anyone in America. No further communications were received that day, but the Valentinos became regular visitors to the seances, where contact was allegedly established with people from the Castellaneta area who had died after Rudy left home.

Under instruction from the medium, the fascinated couple were gradually taught how they could 'communicate directly with the spirit world', and apparently built up a circle of regular contacts who had passed over. Among them: Meselope, an Egyptian born many years before Christ; and Black Feather, an Indian who nominated himself as Valentino's personal spirit 'guide'.

Most of the messages he received were optimistically phrased. One prophesied that his difficulties with Paramount would be resolved before the expiry date of his contract. In another, Black Feather prepared the Valentinos for an extended tour of America, which would bring many new friends and great financial rewards. Both predictions were destined to come true—engineered by a man who at the time was unknown to them both.

It would have taken more than an army of mediums to convince hard-headed public relations man S. George Ullman of the existence of spirits. But had he been consulted, he would have unreservedly endorsed Black Feather's verdict on the Valentinos' immediate future: great financial rewards were just around the corner and he, Sidney George Ullman, was the very man to help the impoverished pair grasp them.

NINETEEN

Will you, won't you, will you, won't you,
Will you join the dance?

Lewis Carroll (1832–98)

CONVINCED THAT THE glamour of the Sheik would bring women in droves to catch even a glimpse of Hollywood's Great Lover, George Ullman had already approached the Mineralava Beauty Clay Company with a startling proposition.

Valentino, he said, may be prevented by the court injunction from appearing in pictures, but there was nothing to stop him going on tour as a dancer. And if the woman who partnered him was Natacha Rambova, and they could be persuaded to endorse the product publicly, it could be the greatest sales gimmick in promotional history.

The directors of the ladies' toiletries firm enthusiastically agreed. Valentino's biography, serialised in *Photoplay*, was creating record sales for the magazine, and as a result Paramount had rebooked all his earlier films in hundreds of theatres around the country. So a personal tour by Valentino could not fail to be a smash hit with his fans. Ullman left Mineralava's offices with a firm commitment in his pocket. They would pay 7,000 dollars a week to the couple—the highest fee ever paid to a dance team—for a four-month cross-country tour of the United States.

Having done his homework well, and knowing the Valentinos' financial position, Ullman anticipated little difficulty in persuading the couple to accept the deal. In early March he boarded a train for Chicago where, now that the California divorce decree was final, Valentino and Natacha were planning to marry. But when he arrived, the public relations man heard that even this arrangement had had to be postponed: Illinois required one year's waiting period after a divorce became final before a marriage licence could be issued.

Despite the turmoil brought by this latest unexpected setback to their wedding plans, Valentino and Natacha agreed to see Ullman in their hotel suite. For Ullman it was an impressive meeting—as he recorded in his diary. It read like a Press release: 'Naturally I was familiar with his pictures and thought of him as a handsome boy. I had no idea of his magnetism, nor of the fine quality of his manhood. To say that I was enveloped by his personality with the first clasp of his sinewy hand and my first glance into his inscrutable eyes is to state it mildly. I was literally engulfed, swept off my feet, which is unusual between two men. Had he been a beautiful woman and I a bachelor, it would not have been so surprising. I am not an emotional man. I have, in fact, often been referred to as cool-headed; but in this instance, meeting a real he-man, I found myself moved by the most powerful personality I had ever encountered in man or woman.'

Valentino, for his part, was immediately interested in Ullman's proposal and impressed by his business shrewdness in arriving with a ready-signed offer from the sponsor. It was a much harder task to convince Natacha that such a promotional tour would not be beneath her dignity. But Valentino had two strong points in his argument to accept: firstly the company they were to pro-

135

mote was in the cosmetics industry, as was her stepfather; secondly, on an all-expense-paid tour, they could use the 7,000 dollars a week to clear their debts and still end up with money in the bank. Enough, he said, to pay for their belated honeymoon to Europe. Natacha surrendered, almost gracefully. The financial argument was one she clearly understood and she also recognised the need to keep her husband-to-be in the public eye until the Paramount injunction expired.

A few days later on March 14, 1923, in the presence of Natacha's aunt Theresa Werner and George Ullman, the couple were married in a secret ceremony at Crown Point, Indiana. At least now they could end the sham of pretending to sleep in separate rooms, laughed Valentino.

After the ceremony they travelled to Chicago once more and boarded the private and luxurious railroad car Ullman had engaged for the tour. It was furnished with gilt mirrors, Turkish carpets, original paintings and carefully-selected furniture. There were private bathrooms and two guest bedrooms, in addition to the newlyweds' main nuptial chamber, and they had their own chef and waiter for the small dining salon.

Valentino was excited and impressed by Ullman's show of concern for their comfort, and even Natacha grudgingly admitted that it bettered her expectations by a considerable margin.

Bad weather was predicted for the first stop on their tour, and Ullman was privately concerned that, now the moment of truth had arrived, his glowing prediction of the reception the Valentinos could expect might have been overly optimistic. True to the forecast, a fierce blizzard was raging in Omaha, Nebraska, when the train carrying the dancers pulled into the main station. Some of the streets were deep with snow and a police escort reported that outlying suburbs were virtually cut off from the town centre. While the couple rested in the honeymoon suite of the main hotel, Ullman anxiously waited at the large auditorium.

He need not have worried. An hour before the performance was due to begin, the theatre was packed to capacity. Hundreds of people, braving the elements to see the Great Lover in person, had to be turned away. As it was, when the orchestra struck up the overture, every aisle in the theatre was packed with standing fans, who cheered wildly as the curtain rose and revealed Valentino in gaucho costume, and Natacha in a Spanish flamenco dress, gliding across the stage in the first steps of a tango.

This initial success was repeated in every town on their itinerary. Huge crowds gathered at the stations for their arrival and departure, theatre managers all reported record attendances, and several city mayors even closed schools to allow the children to see Valentino. Often, when their timetable was published in sufficient detail in advance, admirers lined the railroad track to wave to the couple as their train passed by.

The theatre programme, agreed between Ullman and Valentino in Chicago, never varied. After the initial dances, Rudy would call for silence and thank the Mineralava Company for making his visit to the town possible. His beautiful new wife used the company's beauty products, he declared, and he hoped ladies in the audience would do the same and discover just how helpful the toiletries could be.

A popular feature of the show was a beauty contest, conducted by Valentino, which promised the winner the chance of a movie contract. At the start of the tour, the contest was judged solely by Rudy, but there were so many complaints of favouritism and 'fixing' that Ullman advised a change of format. For the rest of the tour, the contest winners were decided by the audiences themselves and judged on the volume of applause. Each performance ended with Valentino and Natacha re-enacting the scene from *The Four Horsemen* which had made him famous, and gliding off to the film's theme music, *Tango of the Flowers*.

The live performances, and the reissue of his old movies, attracted the largest audiences in history in many towns across America, and the Press reacted by devoting endless pages to the couple's movements, comments and clothes.

But the response which brought most pleasure to Valentino was the public's acceptance of his book *Day Dreams*, a volume of love poems said to have been written by him for Natacha during the year that marriage was denied them. It sold in hundreds of thousands. Outside cinemas, huge placards urged women to enter and thrill to the exploits of the greatest lover of them all, and *Day Dreams* was an extension of that exotic and seemingly irresistible enticement. For while a female admirer had to share her idol with other members of a cinema audience, with *Day Dreams* she could retreat to the privacy of her bedroom and read his words, imagining that he was there, speaking them just for her.

In the preface to the book, also penned by Valentino, they could read: 'To you my gentle reader, I wish to say a foreward of warning before you peruse the contents of this book. I am not a poet nor a scholar, therefore you shall find neither poems nor prose. Just dreams—Day Dreams—a bit of romance, a bit of sentimentalism, a bit of philosophy, not studied, but acquired by constant observation of the greatest of masters! ... Nature!

'While lying idle, not through choice, but because forcibly kept from my preferred and actual field of activity, I took to dreams to forget the tediousness of worldly strife and the boredom of jurisprudence's pedantic etiquette.

'Happy indeed I shall be if my Day Dreams will bring you as much enjoyment as they brought to me in the writing.'

Convinced that Valentino was a natural medium, Natacha maintained that many of the pieces in the volume were inspired by Walt Whitman, Robert and Elizabeth Browning, and other romantically-minded poets. Her husband admitted to being mildly psychic and did not deny that the inspiration for his writings could have come from the spirit world. Dictated from 'the other side' or emanating directly from Valentino's own thoughts, the end result was the same: *Day Dreams* was a runaway success. Three pieces achieved special popularity and were frequently quoted.

In *You*, Valentino seemed to speak directly to the mortal object of his affection—which his adoring fans immediately accepted as themselves:

You are the History of Love and its Justification.
The Symbol of Devotion.
The Blessedness of Womanhood.
The Incentive of Chivalry.
The Reality of Ideals.
The Verity of Joy.
Idolatry's Defence.
The Proof of Goodness.
The Power of Gentleness.
Beauty's Acknowledgment.
Vanity's Excuse.

The Promise of Truth.
The Melody of Life.
The Caress of Romance.
The Dream of Desire.
The Sympathy of Understanding.
My Heart's Home.
The Proof of Faith.
Sanctuary of my Soul.
My Belief in Heaven.
Eternity of All Happiness.
My Prayers.
You.

Valentino's personal involvement with spiritualism had made him far more aware of the ephemeral nature of man's time on earth and this was apparent in *Dust to Dust*.

I take a bone—I gaze at it in wonder—You,
O bit of strength that was. In you today I
see the white sepulcher of nothingness—but
you were the shaft that held together the
vehicle of Man until God called and the Soul
answered.

His *A Baby's Skin* is one of the pieces Natacha claimed was dictated by one of the dead writers who were regular communicants with Valentino:

Texture of a butterfly's wing
Coloured like a dawned rose,
Whose perfume is the breath of God,
Such is the web wherein is held
The treasure of the treasure chest,
The priceless gift—the Child of Love.

140

It was after another message-gathering session with the old Egyptian Meselope and his Indian spirit guide Black Feather, that Valentino approached George Ullman during a stop in the tour at San Antonio, Texas, and asked him to become his personal manager. He was, he said, very impressed with the smooth handling of the Mineralava contract, and the resourcefulness shown by the public relations man in the day-to-day organisation of the tour.

He also admitted that his financial affairs were in a hopeless mess: he owed more than 60,000 dollars, had put his future film career in jeopardy by his wilful and cavalier treatment of Lasky and Paramount, and felt he was being exploited on all sides. Not unnaturally, George Ullman refused to give an immediate answer, but after further begging from Valentino assured him he would seriously consider the proposal. On one point he was adamant: if he accepted Valentino's offer to become his manager, he must have exclusive rights to guide his career and business affairs. There must be no interference from others, especially from Mrs. Valentino.

Valentino considered the implications for only a moment. The immediate problem was to get his affairs in order. What mattered was that his films were raking in millions of dollars, of which he was not receiving a cent, and his debts were growing daily. Lawyers alone were costing him 2,500 dollars a week and they were achieving nothing. If Ullman wanted to operate independently of Natacha, he would have to learn to control her in his own way. Whatever Rudy said now would be invalidated by Natacha's own actions later. He nodded his head.

As soon as the tour ended the Valentinos and George Ullman headed back for New York. Ullman's first task was to pay off Rudy's lawyers and engage someone a good deal cheaper and more effective. He also settled the debt to Joseph Schenck, head of United Artists, and other prominent film executives in Hollywood who had loaned Valentino money during the lean period after his break with Paramount.

Having lifted some of the financial pressure from his new clients, Ullman turned his attention to Valentino's film career.

Ritz-Carlton Pictures, a new movie company with a group of millionaire backers, wanted him to star in a series of films, and J. D. Williams, the president, told Ullman he was prepared to leave the choice of films and director to the star. He had talked with Jesse Lasky at Paramount and, provided Valentino was prepared to make two further films for his contractual employers in the autumn, they would willingly release him to Ritz-Carlton.

Lasky and Paramount boss Joseph Zukor travelled to New York to negotiate the return of their prodigal star. His new salary of 7,500 dollars a week would commence immediately and he would have absolute freedom to choose the scripts, writers, co-stars and directors. The films would be shot at the company's Long Island studios and Natacha would act as technical adviser. It seemed like a total victory for Valentino.

That afternoon the evening newspapers announced the great lover's return to the screen and a crowd of several thousand, mainly women, massed outside the Valentinos' hotel. It was almost dawn before police reserves managed to clear the streets.

In their suite, Rudy toasted George Ullman's prowess as a manager and then lifted his glass to his wife: 'I am once more the complete Rudolph Valentino,' he said. 'Now, at last, we can begin our honeymoon.'

TWENTY

It is a melancholy truth that even great men have their poor relations.

Charles Dickens (1812–70)

WHEN THE GOOD Cunard ship *Aquitania* slipped into Southampton on the second to last day of July in 1923, Rudolph Valentino stood on deck and looked out on England for the first time with mixed emotions of excited, almost childlike anticipation dulled by a gnawing apprehension.

This was, in theory, to be The Triumphant Voyage, the storybook return of the prodigal, culminating in the homecoming of the hero, with his beautiful new bride, to the town from which he'd set off to find fame and fortune. It was, in fact, to become a journey of minor disasters and major disappointments and domestic disagreements ... and a 'belated honeymoon' on which the bride would refuse, point-blank, to continue and insist on going home to mother.

The start had gone well: hundreds of women mobbed the Valentinos in America eight days before when, with Auntie Werner, they arrived to board the ship and had to fight their way up the gangplank. The voyage had passed smoothly, with the couple receiving star treatment, attentive service and the privacy they asked for as honeymooners.

Yet as he prepared to land in England, confessing to a

fellow traveller that he was so excited he had not slept for three nights, Valentino still wondered and worried about the reception he would receive from the Great British Public. Were they as fanatical as those he had left behind on the docks in America? Had his charisma crossed the Atlantic to win over the allegedly reserved English-woman—and did her men regard his screen cavortings as scathingly as many American men did?

His doubts were partially answered by a small but enthusiastic group of admirers who were waiting to greet him, and by photographers who came on deck to take pictures (of him smiling and waving his grey felt hat in welcome, and of Natacha, wearing a bored and disinterested expression above a long, fur-collared coat to protect her from British summertime, which she knew of from her schooldays in Surrey). The reporters seemed genuinely interested, too: 'I have come over entirely for rest and pleasure,' he told them, and added a phrase he was to regret next day: 'I have not had a decent suit in ten years, and now I am going to try London for some.'

By midnight he was in London, where his fears about an apathetic reception were dispelled completely: more than 1,000 men and women had waited hours for him and Valentino, as delighted to see them as they were to set eyes on their idol, declared it 'the most spontaneous and thrilling greeting I've ever had.' Then he and Natacha drove off to the Carlton Hotel where, with more boyish excitement than historical appreciation, Valentino was told that the suite in which he'd sleep had once been occupied by the King and Queen of Belgium.

Next day, a mighty squad and Fleet Street (then, as now, an impressive and fearsome force to face en masse) descended on his hotel armed with questions, cameras and curiosity. They eyed the Eyetie with cool, pro-

144

fessional interest, missing nothing about this strange new super-hero, from his neat dark suit, cornflower blue shirt with matching shot socks) to the grey-and cream check tie, held in place by an emerald pin. And his wife, sitting quietly by his side, rarely smiling, seldom talking, but, despite that determined set to her jaw, undoubtedly attractive in a currently-fashionable 'Polly' dress made for her in New York.

Valentino, knowing the ways and waywardness of the American Press, treated their English cousins warily. 'I'm very glad to be in London,' he announced, to no-body's surprise. 'I've been wanting to come here all my life, and I'll be here for fifteen days. Then, when I've bought some clothes, we'll go to Paris so that Mrs. Valentino can buy some.'

Natacha allows herself a smile. Next question.

How many suits will you buy here? Valentino waves a hand on which, one reporter notes and scribbles down, are three platinum rings, one with a huge emerald, and reveals his flashy (amethyst) cufflinks. 'Oh, say a dozen or so.' And, just in case that sounds a little overly ostentatious: 'As many as I can afford. There's nowhere in the world like London for men's clothes, and as I have to play well-dressed Continental parts, I look upon the suits as an investment.'

Next question.

Will you dance, as has been rumoured, in public in Britain? Valentino grimaces. 'I have received several offers to dance in London, but I'm not accepting any of them. We can't bear the sound of the word dancing. Who could, after dancing the tango for many months throughout the United States, every night? To dance when one has to dance is not the same thing as dancing when one wants to dance.'

145

Natacha breaks her silence.

'Ever since we were married we have been acting and dancing together and going about in a private car without any privacy. Now I think it's quite time we had our honeymoon.'

Sociological question coming up. How about all that jazz? Valentino knows his subject.

'Jazz, unfortunately, has not yet started to die in the States. Over there, I suppose, they must have something to excite them, since they no longer have liquor. I believe that the dances of the future will have the grace and dignity of the old-fashioned ones. There will be a general return to the beauty of the waltz—the dance that will never go out. But at present I consider that the tango, properly danced, is about the best of the modern dances which, on the whole, are not lovely at all.'

Personal, prying-type question is aimed. How long will your honeymoon last? Valentino ducks it.

'I must be back in New York in October for my lawsuit against the Famous Players. I am dissatisfied with my contract which I signed when I was new to business. I don't like the way my latest pictures have been treated, and I want the right to choose my own stories. And there is a clause in the contract which I consider unfair. It states that if my manner, bearing or form changes detrimentally, the Famous Players can suspend me for a year without salary, and with a ban on working for anyone else. Then, if my manner, bearing or form changes back again, they can add the period of my suspension to the period of the contract. I want to break that contract, and sign another with a different firm.'

With that, the conference is over, and the professional seekers-after-truth retire to stuffy, noisy offices (or, more probably, cool and welcoming hostelries) to compose their thoughts.

They were, on the whole, complimentary. 'Mr. Rudolph Valentino,' wrote the *Evening News* reporter, 'whose face and figure on the film have attracted letters by the hundred thousand from girl admirers in America … is tall and very handsome, in the dark, aquiline, iridescent-eyed manner of Mr. Ivor Novello. He appears to be strangely modest and restrained in the popular conception of screen heroes (and) sat and talked of clothes and contracts and the dedicated art of the kinema, while Mrs. Rudolph Valentino listened with intent expression, and lips gently parted.'

Parting lips also fascinated the *Daily Mail* man. Intrigued by the silent star's voice, he revealed exclusively for the benefit of kinemagoers who'd never been given the chance to hear it: 'Mr. Valentino speaks English more like an Englishman than an American—or rather, an Italian, for he is Italian born.'

Whatever the language or the accent, Valentino swore feelingly when he was confronted with his next visitors: no sooner had the Pressmen left his suite than it was invaded by what seemed to be representatives of every tailoring and men's outfitting establishment in the capital. Reading that he wanted to suit himself in London and knowing that their cloth on his frame would be a worldwide walking advertisement, they swarmed in with samples and suggestions, statistics and smooth-talk.

The silent star sent them packing with a few well-chosen words presented with a tired smile, and then slipped out of the hotel to try to become just another tourist. Despite more Press interviews and business calls, he managed to do just that during his London stay: he and Natacha followed the tourist routes to Windsor Castle, the Tower of London, Hampton Court, the theatre. They lunched with Mr. Benjamin Guinness, purveyor of stout to the populace, and met Lord and Lady Birkenhead and their young daughter, Lady Pamela. They visited Natacha's old school, Leatherhead Court in Epsom, and a kennels, and when they finally left Britain, flying from Croydon to Paris on August 15, the new Valentino family was considerably enlarged by three Pekinese which Natacha just couldn't resist.

The spending (and the dog-collecting) continued in Paris where, apart from picking up more praise, invitations and free meals, Valentino competed with his wife's cash investment in Parish fashion by ordering another new wardrobe of clothes and a superb Voisin open tourer to take them to Natacha's parents' home in Nice. Because it could not be ready for the journey, he graciously accepted the loan of another car from the company. And he was also happy to accept, from Mr. Jacques Herbertot, owner of the Theatre Champs Elysees, another dog—a Doberman-Pinscher.

So, with more luggage and more dogs than they comfortably knew what to do with, the Valentinos set off on the next stage of their journey, which was to take them into that distressing and well-known region familiar to millions who'd travelled it before: the First Big Marital Row. In their case, as in innumerable others, it was arrived at via the all-too-common route of her criticising his driving and him criticising her back-seat commandments.

For Valentino, his newly-acquired car was a thrilling, beautiful toy, and he was determined to test it to the full by driving to Nice over the Alps through Grenoble, and Dijon rather than the simpler way through Lyons. Exhilarated, he sped round the snaking, constantly-curving Alpine roads, smiling at the car's performance, laughing at Natacha's pleas to drive more slowly. 'We've plenty of time. There's no need to hurry,' she told him, sitting with every nerve tensed against the disaster she feared at any moment.

Valentino was too enthralled to listen. 'Don't worry. Relax and enjoy it,' he said. 'I know what I'm doing—I have a distinct flair for speed.'

He spoke too soon. As he swung the car around yet another treacherous bend, misjudging speed and distance badly, Natacha screamed in terror: 'Look out! Look out!' and Valentino braked to a halt with one wheel over a precipice.

They sat there for several seconds in silence, Valentino's face ashen, his hands gripping the steering-wheel so tightly that his knuckles showed white, and Natacha shaking with anger, relief, fury and fright.

'Did you notice,' he asked his wife after a while in a quiet, nervous, voice 'that when I wrenched the wheel round, it wasn't only me? Black Feather leaned over to help give that pull that saved us.'

Natacha was not impressed. 'The gods have nothing to do with driving,' she informed her husband, and once again begged him to drive more carefully. He did, and they arrived safely for their reunion with Natacha's parents at their villa.

After a few days in Nice they set off again, taking with them Mrs. Werner, who had gone ahead of them to join the Hudnuts. Destination: Italy. And home.

It was not the happiest of journeys. At the Customs post, Valentino was disappointed to realise that officials did not recognise him. There were no smiles and handshakes and welcoming greetings for the returning hero. Only a long delay and a charge for taking in too many cigarettes. And then in Genoa, Natacha exhausted and tired after the long drive, succumbed to a minor nervous breakdown. 'I'm afraid she won't be able to come with us all the way,' Valentino told Mrs. Werner. 'All this dirt and dust and my driving are a little too much for her sense of humour.'

Next day, however, she felt better, and the journey continued. Their next stop was in Milan, where Valentino's sister, Maria, was to join them for the rest of the trip. But Maria, worried when they did not turn up on time, had taken a train to Genoa, and they missed each other. After more worries, telephone calls and messages, she eventually met up with them in Milan for an emotional, tear-filled reunion. The women eyed each other with guarded interest: Natacha, meeting her husband's sister for the first time, saw a plain, sensibly-dressed young woman who had obviously not known the better things of life. Maria was astounded to discover that her brother had found this very beautiful, fashion-ably-dressed and worldly-wise girl as a wife.

They talked excitedly, of childhood days, of America, of films, of his success, as the journey continued on its precarious course. It came to a sudden halt as they drove into Bologna at sunset—and into a telegraph pole. 'Look out! Look out!' Natacha screamed again. It was too late. The grey pole had merged into the colour of the road and Valentino had not seen it. 'I was only driving slowly, too,' he cursed as he examined a damaged fender.

Swearing again that he would drive more carefully, Rudolph carried on, across the Apennines and more treacherous roads, to Florence and Pisa and eventually Rome. It was here that Natacha decided enough was enough. 'I am going no farther,' she declared and, des-pite protests and repeated promises of slow, crash-proof driving, she left her husband and went back to Nice and mother.

So it was only Rudolph, Maria and Mrs. Werner who left Rome for Campo Basso and the next emotional reunion—with brother Alberto, his wife and son. Once again, there were long hours of reminiscences, memories, talk of childhood days. But Rudolph was impatient to be off, to be on the way to Castellaneta, and home.

Alberto was far from keen to join him: 'The roads are terrible,' he told his brother. 'Anyway, there's nothing up there to see, not many people you'll want to meet.'

But nothing could stand in the way of Rudolph Valentino and home. Nothing except a couple of burst tyres and an hotel in Taranto, where he complained angrily that there was no bath, and was told by the bewildered management that most other guests used the Turkish bath around the corner. Infuriated, and still annoyed that his name did not carry weight here and get the best attention immediately, he set off on the last stage of his sentimental journey.

*   *   *

The baker's boy, head down, hands thrust deep in his pockets, idly kicked the bleached-white stone down the narrow dirt road, scorched hot and dry by the early-afternoon sun, and the dust flew up at his bare, brown legs.

Could it, would it, he wondered, always be like this—the same, dull, pre-determined routine, day after dreary day, week after wasted week, month after monotonous month, with only feast-days and funerals, Christmas, christenings, marriages, births and deaths to mark the passing of time?

Nothing ever happened in Castellaneta, nothing *ex-*

citing anyway. There wasn't even a cinema to which a boy could go, to gaze, to dream, to wonder at the world outside which just a few fortunate young men of Castellaneta had left home to see. One day he, too, might join them—in America, perhaps. It was something he would think about, something to plan for. But, for today, there was nothing to look forward to. Except siesta, of course. It would be time for that soon.

The boy reached the stone and kicked at it again, more powerfully this time, and watched as it hurtled up and forward and ... something flashed into his vision and he shielded his eyes from the sun to see it better. It was! An automobile. A great, grand, gleaming automobile, the most beautiful and exiting thing he had ever seen, was charging up towards him. Coming into Castellaneta! He watched as it came nearer and noisily nearer and shuddered to a halt in the road where he stood in awe. He heard voices, of a man and two women, inside, and a few moments later a door opened and the man got out and stretched and looked around with a strange look on his face.

He seemed sad, somehow lost, but to the boy he looked absurd, standing there in the middle of the town beside his magnificent machine, with a huge, stylish almost comical cloak wrapped around him. Who could he be? What did he want here? Why had he come?

Laughing excitedly, the boy ran to the big, twelve-room house where the sisters lived. He must tell them.

In the house, Don Angelo Maldarizzi was pottering about. His wife, Donna Vincenza, was in the kitchen with their two daughters, 17-year-old Rita and Ada who was four years younger. Suddenly, the baker's boy burst in. 'Guardate le maschere!' he shouted. 'Guardate le maschere!' Curiously the girls ran to the door to see the

152

'circus clowns' the boy was shouting about, and were, as they told friends next day, 'dumbfounded'. Rita felt her legs go weak, feared she might faint, as she looked at the man in the cloak and saw the boy she had once been so close to, but had almost forgotten—Rodolpho Guglielmi.

One by one the family hugged and embraced the man and then his sister. The boy looked on, wide-eyed and bewildered, at the wild commotion, the excited babble, the laughter and the tears. Even the man was crying. The boy could see the tears on his cheeks. But the other woman, the one he heard say was 'the aunt of my wife' did not join in. She sat in the car the whole time, not understanding what the others were saying.

Eventually they went into the house. Donna Vincenza brewed coffee and brought out cakes, a local speciality Rodolpho loved as a boy, and he lounged back on a divan, smoking, talking, explaining. 'I was in Taranto,' he said, 'and I knew I dare not leave without coming back home. I had to see it. But everything is exactly the same as when I left.' He kept repeating this: 'Nothing has changed at all. Everything is exactly the same.'

He talked of his life, his wife, his films. Rita was dazzled. She had never seen a film, nor heard of Hollywood. He seemed, she thought, to live in a fairyland world. And, she knew, he had changed. He was wholly and totally different from the boy she had known.

Her father saw that too, and suddenly, in a friendly but firm way, began to scold his visitor. 'Why did you have to run off from home, gallivanting abroad? Your place was to remain here, with your family and the people you were raised with.'

Rodolpho sat forward, waving his arms in emphasis. Everything he does, Ada thought, seems to be theatrical. 'But Don Angelo,' he protested, 'you must understand that America has given me millions. Do you realise that? Millions! And I have to be where there are millions. Millions of dollars! Can't you see that?'

Don Angelo shook his head: 'I suppose you know best. The young always do. But it's sad to see young men like you leaving our town. Some of them never come back...'

'But I'm back,' Rodolpho laughed. 'I've come to look at the house, and visit the cemetery. I'll go now.'

He went alone, through the siesta-silenced streets, to stand quietly at the family tomb, and to look at the whitewashed house in which he'd been born and where, with tears and grief he thought would break his heart, he had kissed his mother for the last time before leaving for America. But he had been right to go. He knew that now. This was a distressing, depressing, unchanging town. He could never have been happy here. Even now, few recognised him as a famous man or knew what a great success he had made of his life.

When he returned to the Maldarizzi's home, Rita sensed that he was unhappy, restless. 'You will stay and eat with us?' Donna Vincenza asked. 'We don't know when we will see you again. It may be years...'

'No, no thank you,' he said, motioning to Maria. 'We really must be off...'

'But you will come back, soon ... some day?' Rita asked. Rodolpho smiled. 'Who knows?' he said, and he said it, Ada thought again, like an actor in a drama. And then, with more kisses and embraces, he was gone.

As he climbed into the car, a few people said hello. The word had gone around that he was back. But their greetings were polite rather than warm. He shook their hands, exchanged a few words and drove off.

The sisters cried. They knew they would never see

154

him again. 'What,' Rita asked, 'does the geat Rodolpho want with a little country town with dirt roads and carts?'

The boy watched as the magnificent automobile drove off down the dry dirt road, the way it had come, in the direction of Taranto. He watched until it was just a speck in the distance. Then he turned and walked slowly home. One day, he thought, I might go away and come back in an automobile like that.

If, if only . . .

TWENTY-ONE

My wife hath something in her gizzard,
that only waits an opportunity of being
provoked to bring up.

Samuel Pepys (1633–1703)

THE STORY CHOSEN by Natacha and Valentino for his
dramatic comeback was a fitting one—*Monsieur Beaucaire*, which recounted the daringly amorous activities of
the dashing Duc de Chartres. In pre-publicity interviews,
he promised to be once again the Great Lover, providing
romance and excitement for all.

But to ensure the delivery of the right mixture of passion and beefcake, Lasky called for the original script to
be pepped up and suggested that production of the film
be postponed until the New Year. Delighted when the
company agreed to pay their travel expenses, the Valentinos re-embarked for Europe to spend Christmas with
the Hudnuts at their chateau in Nice.

Anticipating a full-scale American-style celebration,
Rudolph had bought sufficient decorations to fill two
large tea chests, and insisted on the Hudnuts installing a
huge Christmas tree in the hall. They spent most of one
night dressing the tree with dozens of coloured balls,
tinsel, cotton wool snowballs, glittering ornaments,
crackers and gifts. About one hundred candles in clip-on
holders completed the decoration. Mrs. Hudnut was
against lighting the candles, but on Christmas Eve Rudy

156

insisted. Mrs. Hudnut agreed. Anything to keep her son-in-law happy.

Valentino and Natacha, standing on stools, used long tapers to light the candles, and had almost finished when he spotted one towards the back which they had missed. As he reached through the branches, the flame accidentally brushed a snowball and in moments the whole tree was ablaze.

As the others panicked and Valentino dashed out to fetch a hose, Mrs. Werner, unflappable as ever, collected the presents piled near the foot of the tree and moved them to safety. While Mrs. Hudnut screamed for everyone to save her valuable tapestries and furniture, pails of water and Rudy's garden hose finally quenched the blaze. But the festive spirit was dampened and Mrs. Hudnut no longer had the same fondness in her eyes when she looked on her son-in-law.

A week later, he returned to New York and a totally unprecedented display of adulation from his fans.

Absence from the screen in new films had not done any damage to his reputation among his female admirers, and news that he was to film on Long Island had caused a rush on rented properties there. When shooting started, there wasn't a single room to be had within twenty miles of the studio.

Women pleading for just a few moments alone with the star, and the chance to gaze directly into those smouldering eyes, camped outside the studio gates and refused to move. The studio switchboard was flooded with calls, many of them of an extremely intimate nature, and hundreds of letters were delivered daily. Some of the writers enclosed snippets of their undergarments and beseeched Valentino to touch them, preferably with his lips, and return them to the sender. Others enclosed

157

nude photographs and detailed descriptions of what they would do to the lover of their dreams. To be ravished as the Sheik had ravished Diana, without scruple, was their heart's desire. A flattered, but slightly perplexed, Valentino professed amusement in public, but demanded that a round-the-clock bodyguard be provided by Paramount to keep his worshipping fans at arm's distance.

Newspapers and magazines revealed to their readers that Valentino did not confine his amorous activities to the screen. Not all his fans were turned away disappointed, it was hinted. Furiously, Natacha demanded that all reporters be banned from the studio. Paramount executives promised this would be done then secretly ordered the publicity department to leak further 'intimate disclosures' to the gossip writers.

From the day shooting started, Natacha had been in an evil temper, constantly berating her husband both in public and private. She criticised his acting, his posture and his make-up, and because he failed to stand up to her, Valentino earned added criticism from his fellow actors and the film crew. Believing that only Natacha could lift him to the great heights his talent deserved, he was content to let her have her way, and supported her whenever there was opposition to her meddlesome activities around the studio. After each day's filming, she would gather the cast and director Sydney Olcott about her and review their performances, delighting in exercising the authority which the studio had afforded her as part of their settlement with Valentino.

Olcott's protests increased. He told Lasky that Natacha constantly interfered and questioned even his smallest decisions. She was making him virtually redundant. It required all Lasky's persuasive talents to prevent his director walking out, but his pleas to Olcott and everyone

158

associated with the production were successful, and the film was completed only a few days over schedule. For the spectacular production, Paramount had used two assistant directors and more than a score of specialists never before taken on for the making of a movie. These included a director of etiquette, a fencing master, a dancing master and Valentino's private fiddler and poetry reader.

But the extravagant 'extras', provided by the studio to ensure the smooth production of Valentino's comeback picture, did nothing to contain the actor's grandiose ideas and, despite frequent stern warnings from George Ullman, he had begun another period of lavish spending. Most of his purchases were expensive antiques to complete the furnishing of his Whitley Heights house in California, and his expenditure was outpacing his income by several thousand dollars a week. By the last day of filming on *Monsieur Beaucaire*, a disillusioned but wiser Ullman had to inform his irrepressible charge that they were again in debt to Paramount. Valentino was unrepentant.

In August the film opened in New York, to favourable notices from the critics and long queues outside the theatres. *Variety* predicted that women would go for this one in their thousands. Initially at least, it seemed that Valentino was still the greatest box-office attraction in America, even after a two year lay-off.

Certainly Douglas Fairbanks was unable to compete when his latest film, *Thief of Bagdad*, opened in New York soon afterwards. Forty-Sixth Street was mobbed with people who wanted to see Fairbanks and Mary Pickford arrive for the premiere.

The two superstars planned to have everyone seated before making their entrance and thought they were the last to arrive. But, half a block from the theatre, Fairbanks heard the excited screams of hundreds of women. Lowering his car's window, he heard cries of 'We love you Rudy!' and 'Rudy, you're wonderful!' from the ecstatic fans as Rudolph Valentino made his entrance into the theatre.

No-one could follow that, Fairbanks decided. After the reception the great lover had just been given, he and Mary would be an anti-climax. Grabbing his equally-daunted co-star, he hurled himself on the floor of the limousine and shouted to the chauffeur to make another tour of the block.

Meanwhile, inside the theatre, Rudy swept through the lobby and, to deafening cheers, strode to the first box. All around, women in the first night audience were in confusion. Men were staring in open envy at the handsome Italian who, with professional modesty, bowed slightly and sat down, eyes fixed on the screen—waiting quietly for the lights to go down and the picture to begin.

Only after the orchestra had struck up the theme music and the first images were flickering on the screen did Mary Pickford and Douglas Fairbanks creep into the darkened theatre through the stage door. Valentino had completely stolen their glory.

But his popularity with the people at Paramount remained in direct proportion to the amount of time he was accompanied by Natacha. Valentino alone, they loved. Valentino with his wife had become an unacceptable package. No amount of success with *Monsieur Beaucaire* could persuade the Natacha-worn Sydney Olcott to direct another Valentino picture if the 'she devil', as he had dubbed her, retained any kind of authority.

Joseph Henaberry was brought in to replace him for Valentino's last film with the studio, a South American

Valentino's bigamy trial: Rudy listens as his lawyers confer.

Above and below Valentino's Hollywood home, Whitley Heights. *Opposite* Castellaneta, where he was born.

Valentino shortly before his death.

RUDY'S DEATH occupied the whole front page of many newspapers on Monday, 13 August, 1926. The 'Los Angeles Record' noted: 'Death came at 12.10 p.m.' The newspaper spotlighted Pola Negri's grief: 'Unconscious and hysterical by turns . . . Pola Negri, reported fiancee of the dead film star, was under the care of two physicians in her Ambassador Hotel bungalow today.' Sceptics hinted she was merely seeking publicity.

Above The body leaves the hospital. *Below* The lying-in-state.

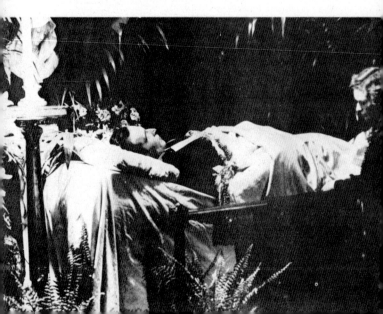

Above The body was viewed by an incredible 50,000 people per day. *Below* A shrine was opened in Castellaneta.

adventure story adapted from Rex Beach's novel *Rope's End*, to be retitled *A Sainted Devil*. To demonstrate her authority to the end, Natacha personally chose the two leading ladies, Nita Naldi and Jetta Goudal.

Jetta, a beautiful and talented French actress, was captivated by Valentino's striking looks and Continental charm, and made no secret of her off-screen interest in him. He considered it harmless to indulge in a light flirtation, but reckoned without his wife's jealousy and, worse, her incredible pride. That Rudy should publicly show even the slightest interest in any woman other than herself was considered a direct insult by his fiery spouse.

The young Frenchwoman's days on the picture were numbered, and the incident which clinched her premature departure came during an inspection of the costumes, which Natacha had designed. Jetta stared incredulously at the clothes and burst out laughing. They must be intended for effeminate men and deformed women, she shrieked. Jetta Goudal would never allow herself to be photographed in these ridiculous garments.

Natacha stormed from the set, her mouth twisted in a snarl, and next morning it was announced that Miss Goudal had been dismissed from the cast for indiscipline. Her place would be taken by Valentino's good (and platonic) friend Dagmar Godowsky.

As filming of *A Sainted Devil* proceeded, complaints about Natacha again began pouring in to Jesse Lasky's office, and he estimated that, if anything, she had exceeded her previous power-play schemings. Paramount's Vice President praised God that this was the last occasion he would be called upon to adjudicate between the Valentinos and his other employees, and with skill accumulated from long practice, smoothed the ruffled feathers of his director and assistants, and advised that the sooner they finished the picture the sooner they would be rid of Natacha. On the set the unceasingly henpecked star silently suffered his wife's tantrums and criticism and was always ready to agree when she scolded one of the other actors or clashed with the director and technicians.

It seemed to outsiders as though Natacha desperately wanted to prove she was more important to the picture than her husband, and that he was quite prepared for this to be so. Whatever the reasons, he endured her harangues with smiles and fortitude. Surprisingly, the film was completed without another major incident. 'Miraculously' was how Jesse Lasky put it as he beamed across at Paramount President Adolph Zukor and toasted the departure of their 'Number One Headache'. Natacha had now become the problem of J. D. Williams and his unfortunate colleagues at the virgin Ritz-Carlton studios.

Williams's first inkling of what lay ahead came during their first meeting to discuss Valentino's debut picture. He was informed by Natacha that she, and she alone, knew how to exploit her husband's talents. To that end she had written a thrilling screen story of love and war in medieval Spain under the pseudonym Justice Layne. The dumbfounded studio boss was then told that Natacha intended to direct the picture, to be retitled *The Hooded Falcon* from her original story, *The Scarlet Power*, and she would also design all sets and all costumes.

Valentino nodded his agreement as Natacha went on to explain how they intended making a tour of Spain to purchase authentic costumes and props and do further research. The cornered Williams, faced with the combined personalities of the formidable pair, could only mumble his consent, though he added an earnest plea that they keep their expenses down to a maximum of fifty thousand dollars.

Natacha's scornful answering look to this request should have warned him. The plundering expedition to Spain was to be carried out in truly lavish Valentino style.

TWENTY-TWO

Never meddle with playactors
For they're a favoured race.

Miguel Cervantes (1547–1616)

THE SACKING OF SPAIN, as J. D. Williams came to call the Valentinos' jaunt across the Iberian peninsula, set the studio back a little over one hundred thousand dollars. As the spendthrift couple swooped on town after town, leaving stunned but substantially richer antique merchants in their wake, they were pursued by a series of telegrams, each more belligerent than the last, demanding they curb their spending and confine themselves to buying only necessities for the forthcoming production.

But these missives from New York served only to spur the 'researchers' on to new heights of extravagance. Fresh crates of antique armour, weapons and furnishings, carpets, tapestries and costumes, matador outfits and mantillas, books, paintings and ornaments were despatched daily to America. Finally, in a state of near exhaustion from their efforts, the Valentinos and Natacha's mother arrived in Seville, where they accepted an invitation to the Sunday bullfight.

Recalling his own endeavours in the ring during the filming of *Blood and Sand*, Valentino temporarily slipped back into his role of Juan Gallardo and made an entrance every bit as impressive and arrogant as the three matadors who were to face the afternoon's quota of bulls. Sit-

164

ting below the President's box, the two women were treated to a running commentary on the action by a highly-excited Valentino, who at one stage had to be physically restrained from leaping into the ring and assisting in the despatching of one of the magnificent animals.

'This is real man's work!' he yelled. 'Making films is only for cissies.'

Only the prompt intervention of two stern-faced policemen prevented his breaking free from his wife and mother-in-law to join the matadors, but afterwards he insisted on being taken to their disrobing room to congratulate the heroes on their performance. During their return train ride to Nice he spoke enthusiastically of giving up his film career and devoting himself to the Corrida de Toros, and on arrival at the Hudnut villa could scarcely contain himself until a projector had been set up and he was able to watch a private copy of *Blood and Sand*.

Among themselves, the Hudnuts and their other guests admitted they preferred *Monsieur Beaucaire*, but in front of Valentino they praised his skill in portraying the courage of Gallardo so convincingly, and managed to stifle their yawns as the film was screened six times in one weekend.

Ignoring several new appeals from J. D. Williams to speed their return to America, the couple decided to tour the château region of France to enable Natacha to make further studies of fourteenth-century European costume. Valentino, under his wife's prompting, used the period to grow a small but distinguished-looking beard which, with make-up to darken his olive skin even further, would make him a very convincing Moorish lord, she said.

165

Eventually the cables from New York became so ominously emphatic that even Natacha felt they could no longer disregard them and they set sail for America in the *Leviathan*. On arrival they were met with disappointing news from a rather disgruntled J. D. Williams: June Mathis was having difficulties with the script of *The Hooded Falcon*, and it had also been decided that, because of lack of studio space in New York, the film would have to be made on the West Coast.

The whole studio, therefore, was being moved to Hollywood. Valentino and Natacha found it difficult to argue. If they wanted the picture to be made on the lavish scale they had envisaged, they must have the necessary space. Williams also warned that the picture would not be able to absorb all the articles they had bought in Spain, and some of them might have to be considered their private acquisitions.

While they digested this piece of news, Williams revealed that because preparation of *The Hooded Falcon* might well run into many more weeks, he had bought the film adaptation of *Cobra*, a successful Broadway stage play. This could go into immediate production, he said, and as his backers in Ritz-Carlton were becoming restless at the delay in seeing a return on their investment, he urged them both to accept.

'But do we have your promise that *The Hooded Falcon* will be next?' Natacha asked.

'Certainly,' replied Williams. 'You have my word on it.'

'In that case Rudy will do *Cobra*,' said Natacha, and to Williams' intense surprise and relief—he had heard disturbing reports about the shrewish Mrs. Valentino's interference in production—she added: 'I will have no part in the filming of it. This is the kind of modern story that bores me to tears. I will concentrate on the designs for *Falcon*.'

Meanwhile Valentino's arrival in New York with a beard had caused a storm of protest among his admirers—and Paramount, seeing a fresh source of publicity in the controversy to help launch *A Sainted Devil*, contacted the American Master Barbers' Association. If Valentino kept his beard, wives all over the country would urge their husbands to follow suit, they warned.

The great lover's goatee became a subject for hot debate among the country's barbers and the Association passed a resolution declaring that its members were pledged, along with their families and friends, not to attend showings of Rudolph Valentino's pictures as long as he remained bewhiskered.

The male population, they said, was likely to be guided by the actor to the extent of making beards fashionable again, and such a fashion would not only injure their trade, but would utterly deface America and make its citizens difficult to distinguish from Russians.

Bowing to the demands of his fans, and the barbers, Rudy submitted to having his beard shaved. (It had, he admitted later, caused him a good deal of discomfort, anyway).

It was almost two years since the couple had bought their house on Whitley Heights, and now they were to have their first opportunity to live in it.

Several tons of furniture had been despatched there in the intervening period and most of it was now found to be totally unsuitable. Only the best items were kept and the rest was sent off to be auctioned, at a fraction of its original cost, or placed in storage. And that was not the only problem : Natacha, far from being satisfied with her new home, complained that it was much too small for their needs and demanded that Valentino find something more appropriate.

Despite her dissatisfaction over the size of the house, Natacha seemed to be making a genuine effort to please her husband during the first months after their return to Hollywood. Her present to him that Christmas was to become one of the most talked-about gifts from any woman to any man since the days of Mark Antony and Cleopatra.

She designed the present herself and sent their handy-man and friend, Mahoney, to Tiffanys with the drawings. Meanwhile Valentino was planning his own surprise. Recalling how much she had admired a diamond-studded locket watch at the time of their engagement, he asked George Ullman to visit the jewellers and, if it were still for sale, buy it.

At six o'clock on Christmas morning, Natacha phoned Ullman and invited him to drive immediately round to the house with his wife and their six-year-old son, Danny. When they arrived, Natacha was waiting outside and kept them talking until a shout came from inside that all was ready. Valentino met them in the hall and led them through to the living room where, covering the entire black marble floor, was a network of railroad tracks, tunnels, houses, electric switches, rail and passenger cars, platforms and level crossings. It was laid out like the main rail terminal of a large city and had cost Valentino a small fortune. It was, he said, a present for Daniel in appreciation of the work Ullman had done for Natacha and himself.

Natacha revealed that he had spent the entire night assembling the set—and caught a cold sitting on the bare marble floor. But Daniel's happiness in operating the giant layout more than compensated for all his efforts, and Rudy, she chided, had enjoyed himself putting the terminal together almost as much as in presenting it. Fortunately he had something to do, she confided to Ullman, because they had quarrelled furiously on Christmas Eve and had barely spoken to each other until the family arrived.

Any last remaining effects of the quarrel were quickly dispelled when Natacha produced her special gift for her husband—a platinum slave bracelet, which she solemnly placed on Rudy's wrist. Recognising the symbolism of it, he took Natacha in his arms and kissed her passionately, oblivious of the embarrassed stares of the Ullmans. Declaring his slavery to her beauty and kindliness, Valentino swore that he would never remove the bracelet. Though it later aroused heated controversy among his fans, and a sneering attack in the Press, he never went back on this promise.

Then it was Valentino's turn to present his gift. When Natacha opened the white velvet case and saw the jewel he had bought her, she hurled herself back into his arms. For the remainder of their married life, she rarely removed it from her wrist.

The weeks that followed were among the happiest Valentino could remember. He was in peak condition, and rarely arrived on the set of *Cobra* later than six o'clock. The prizefight scenes in the picture enabled him to show off his physique, and he was overwhelmed when Williams announced that world heavyweight boxing champion Jack Dempsey had agreed to act as technical advisor and would give him lessons in boxing. After one of their regular sparring sessions, Dempsey joked that if Valentino ever decided to quit acting and turn to boxing, professional fighters would be in for a tough time.

Playing the part of an Italian count, Valentino could be

himself for the first time on film. After his early morning bouts at the studio with sparring partner Gene Delment, who was appearing frequently at the American Legion Stadium in Hollywood, he would drive himself home in his high-powered Voisin, and reappear an hour later after breakfasting.

Cheering news came from George Ullman, who had discovered a Mediterranean style house in Bella Drive, overlooking Beverly Hills, which met with Natacha's approval.

The gardens, eight and three-tenths acres of scenic hilltop, were beautifully landscaped with nearly fifty trees, mostly Italian Cypress, and many rare European and Oriental shrubs. The house, an Italian Spanish stucco type with red tiled roof, was constructed on two levels. The sixteen rooms included three master bedrooms, three bathrooms, servant's room, wardrobe room, film laboratory and laundry room on the lower level, and on the upper level, a library, small office, large living room, dining room, kitchen, cook's and butler's pantries, a servant's ante room and a large reception room with adjoining cloak and washroom. There was a garage for four cars, with six rooms above it as servants' quarters, stables large enough to accomodate four horses, and kennels for twelve dogs next to the groom's quarters. The house, built the previous year, was going for 175,000 dollars, including undeveloped land adjoining the property.

Joseph Schenck agreed to stand behind the purchase and Ullman obtained the deeds. In honour of Natacha's film, declared Rudolph, they would rename the house Falcon's Lair. But Natacha was not impressed. After an idyllic few weeks, she had reverted to form and the couple's quarrels became increasingly vicious. Friends who had taken to calling at the Whitley Heights house now no longer came. They could not face the embarrassment of watching Valentino endure his wife's violent, destructive tirades. She questioned his prowess as an actor, an artist and as a lover. He was, she accused, too spineless to fight for decent roles in decent pictures. He was a fool with his talent, with his money and with his choice of friends, who, she rightly claimed, loathed her.

Details of their quarrels were inevitably repeated, and just as inevitably ended up in the gossip columns. Did the slave bracelet force him to accept all Madame Valentino's outbursts without retaliation? asked the columnists. But this only made him more defensive of his wife in public—and made her more bitter towards himself and his friends, whom she now barred from the house, not appearing to notice that they had voluntarily stopped visiting.

Adding to Valentino's misery were reports from the cutting room that they had a disaster on their hands. The chief cameraman had quit early in the production and the second cameraman had failed to adapt to the same style. Joe Henaberry, who had managed to salvage a reasonable finished product from *A Sainted Devil*, had failed to come through with *Cobra*. Nita Naldi and Valentino played their roles as though half asleep, and the only time the great lover came to life was in the boxing sequences. Natacha's insistence on changes in the story had also removed what little plot existed.

Depressed by this news, and yearning for a less stormy matrimonial condition, Valentino insisted that Natacha take off with him for Palm Springs and a short holiday away from the studios, their friends and the snipers of the gossip columns. He had often talked of the time babies would be in his home, and now he believed the one certain road to her heart, the condition that would soften her temper and turn her frowns to smiles, was motherhood.

Natacha was appalled. 'How can we have children when you are living the kind of life you do?' she snapped. 'I will start having babies when you stop being an actor. Not until. It's nonsense to think of starting a family when we are in this abnormal profession.'

Valentino was saved from having to answer by a telephone call from George Ullman in Hollywood. J. D. Williams had disowned them. With hefty criticism of his star, whom he claimed showed a distinct lack of manliness in facing up to his wife, he had announced the liquidation of Ritz-Carlton. Pre-production costs of *The Hooded Falcon* had been written off as a total loss and Williams was going out of picture making. What could have been a prosperous and lasting partnership between Valentino and the studio had been ruined by their irresponsible behaviour.

Chastened, the Valentinos rushed back to Hollywood for a meeting with their business manager. Natacha immediately began to denounce the Ritz-Carlton syndicate, but Ullman cut her off brusquely. Perhaps, he reminded her, a little less of her voice in the past might have placed her husband in a much stronger position to deal with the studios.

But all was not lost. United Artists were prepared to sign a contract with Rudy that would bring him more than one million dollars a year. This, on condition they agreed to one, special clause: Natacha would not be permitted to have a voice in the selection of material, cast, design, staging or the employment of director and other technical assistants.

In fact, she would be allowed no official connection with any part of his pictures, and Joseph Schenck per-

172

sonally had said he would prefer it if Natacha did not even enter the studio gates.

Natacha's face contorted. 'Rudy will never sign a contract like that,' she declared. 'He knows he is totally unable to perform unless I am there to advise him. No-one understands him as I do. Who can chose the right material to further his career if I can have no hand in it? He's incapable of doing it himself.'

Valentino leapt to his feet and, taking his wife by the shoulders, pushed her down into her chair. 'You have cost me my friends and humiliated me in public,' he shouted. 'You have mocked my work and abused my talent. But this time I will do things my way. Your job is to have babies. My job is to make films. And that is what I am going to do.'

He turned to an astonished George Ullman and told him: 'Tell Mr. Schenck I am prepared to sign a contract on those terms immediately.'

TWENTY-THREE

Now the peak of summer's past, the sky is overcast
And the love we swore would last for an age seems
deceit.

C. Day-Lewis (1904–72)

NATACHA RAMBOVA, if nothing else, possessed a well-developed sense of timing and a well-honed ability to judge her husband's emotional moods and manipulate him accordingly. Valentino's taunt about her role in life being confined to breeding his heirs had, not surprisingly in view of her reluctance to start a family, failed to strike an answering chord in her far-from-maternal breast.

But, with characteristic cunning, she waited until his own stepping-stone to future greatness—a signed contract with Schenck—had materialised before revealing her own formula for virtuosity in the motion picture industry. The crowning recognition of Valentino's talent as an actor debarred her from any participation in his glorification, but did not infuse her with any degree of enthusiasm. To Natacha, only one person's achievements mattered. Her own.

Elated after his latest meeting with Schenck, Valentino returned to Whitley Heights bubbling with news of his first project for United Artists. The studio chief had revealed he was to star in *The Eagle*, a film adaptation of Alexander Pushkin's *Dubrovsky*. This costume role as a daring and amorous Russian Robin Hood, in the same

174

mould as the Sheik, delighted Valentino. United Artists had also secured Vilma Banky, the blonde Hungarian beauty discovered by Sam Goldwyn in Budapest, to be his leading lady.

His inwardly fuming wife, who had recently been living up to her old Hollywood nickname of 'The Icicle', embraced him warmly and led him to a double settee, where a fresh drink—a glass of chilled white wine—was waiting for him on a side table. Her revealing gown and jewelled turban were further evidence of a well-rehearsed scenario, but the overjoyed Rudolph was in too euphoric a mood to notice. Since Ullman's bombshell she had been frostily polite in public and ominously silent in private. This new mood, he thought, augured well for the future.

In his hand he clutched a sheaf of cablegrams from the founding stars of United Artists, Charlie Chaplin, Mary Pickford, Douglas Fairbanks and Norma Talmadge, welcoming him to 'the team'. On top of everything else, he told her, instead of a dressing room he was being provided with a luxuriously-fitted bungalow, a personal chef and dresser.

'At last I have found someone who will treat me as a star,' he told Natacha. 'This will be the greatest film I have ever made. It will make me a millionaire.' For, in addition to a salary of more than half a million dollars a year, United Artists had granted him forty-two per cent of profits on his films.

'And I am to have no part of it?' asked Natacha.

Valentino stared at her, his guilt clearly written across his handsome features. 'But with this I can provide you with anything you want,' he said.

It was what she had been waiting for. Quickly, before his guilt evaporated, she outlined her own project,: if she could not work with him, she would become an independent producer and make her own pictures. She would write the stories herself and direct stars like Nita Naldi and Nazimova, who would willingly support her project. Frantically, Valentino backpedalled, suddenly aware of the silken noose he had helped place around his own neck. But Natacha pressed home her advantage, using all the feminine wiles and persistent argument—for which she was notorious. Her first film, she revealed, would be a satirical tale of the agonies suffered by women in the beauty parlour, to be called *What Price Beauty?*

Eventually, as she knew he must, Valentino yielded and instructed George Ullman to make fifty thousand dollars available to Natacha, who immediately signed Nita Naldi to star in her picture and doubled the cost of production. At least, Rudy told his manager, it kept her happy while he got on with the business of making *The Eagle*.

But separate careers, one still in the ascendancy and the other predestined for failure, did not provide the magical solution to their domestic problems that Valentino was seeking. From the time Natacha began making her own films, she became even more possessed by her passion to be a power in the motion picture world.

Reported George Ullman: 'When her dictatorship was taken from her, it was not long before her loyalty to Valentino, not only to his business interests, but to him as a wife, began to fail her. When she ceased to collaborate, she also failed to co-operate—in more ways than one.'

By early August, Falcon's Lair was ready for occupation, but Natacha refused to make the move. She refused to even visit the house, and deliberately made a point of being out with friends when Valentino came home to Whitley Heights. Her bad temper was partly due to her being unable to find a distributor for *What Price Beauty?* and, declaring that only in the East could she arrange for release of her picture, she informed Valentino that she was moving to New York.

Failing to dissuade her, he insisted she take George Ullman to act as a business advisor, and on August 13, a prophetically unlucky day to begin their separation, Valentino drove his wife to the station in their new Isotta-Fraschini. Crowds turned out to see the departure and Press photographers pushed each other aside to snatch pictures of the couple's farewell kiss. No-one knew it at the time, but it was to be their last.

Looking sad and depressed, Valentino followed her on to the platform and, as the train pulled away, began walking, then running, alongside her compartment. Then he stood alone, waving, until the train disappeared around a curve in the track, and turned and walked slowly, head bowed, to his car.

Opposite Natacha in the drawing room of their private suite, Ullman asked: 'Do you love Rudy?'

She shook her head. 'I don't know,' she whispered.

'Do you want to go back to him,' asked the concerned manager.

'I don't know,' she said again.

'Do you want a divorce and lose Rudy out of your life forever?' he persisted.

'I don't know,' choked Natacha, and burst into tears.

Hardly had the couple separated than the Press began hinting at a serious rift in their stormy marriage. Her statement to one newspaper that 'this marital vacation will be a good thing for us both' shocked Valentino. Desperately he tried to reach her on the telephone, but the number in her apartment did not answer. A frantic exchange of telegrams with George Ullman did nothing to ease his anxiety.

Natacha, Ullman reported, had asked him to find her a part for her in a picture, and he had secured a role in a film called, fittingly, *When Love Grows Cold*.

Valentino countered Press speculation with a statement that Natacha had no intention of sueing for divorce. Their separation, he said, was due to a difference in temperament.

'We have been happy together and may be again,' he announced. 'I am sorry that this had to happen, but we cannot always order our lives the way we would like to have them.'

To combat the sadness of the separation, Valentino sought solace in the company of Vilma Banky, his co-star, and they began appearing regularly together in public, at parties, film openings and society gatherings. Rumours of a passionate love affair between the two stars of *The Eagle* were steadfastly denied by both Valentino and Miss Banky, but the newspapers gave the supposed romance considerable coverage, which did not find favour with Natacha, who by this time was in France, visiting her mother and buying clothes for her forthcoming film.

Newspapers also carried the story that Imre Lukatz, the Hungarian nobleman to whom Vilma Banky had been engaged before leaving her homeland for America, had threatened to kill the great lover if they ever came face to face.

Another sneering statement from Natacha brought a comment from her husband that she could not appear in pictures and be his wife at the same time. She must choose which she preferred. He did not know if they would be reconciled or divorced, but she could not return as his wife if she wished to pursue a career.

In November Valentino travelled to New York for the opening of *The Eagle* and was mobbed at every stop. In New York he had to be provided with a five-strong bodyguard to walk the few yards from his hotel to a waiting limousine. Everywhere he appeared, vast crowds gathered to scream and cheer, and on the second day police reserves were called in and detailed to travel with the star for the rest of his stay in the city. On the day *The Eagle* opened, at the Mark Strand Theatre, thousands of fans queued all day in the hope of getting seats, but when the box office closed several thousands were still waiting outside. On his arrival, Valentino was given a tumultuous reception which even that city had rarely witnessed, and when the film had been shown, the audience stamped and cheered until he appeared on stage. The standing ovation he received after thanking his admirers for their kindness lasted several minutes, and, eyes blinded by tears, he had to be helped from the stage. The critics were no less enthusiastic in their report of the star's performance, and everywhere *The Eagle* played to packed houses.

Joseph Schenck had proved that with the right picture and the right director—and without the meddlesome, interfering presence of Natacha Rambova—Valentino was still the undisputed box office champion.

On November 10, 1925 Valentino applied for American citizenship. On the same day, Natacha returned from Europe, but the two did not meet. She refused to comment on divorce rumours but, asked if she considered a sheik an ideal husband, she retorted: 'I can't say. I have never been married to a sheik.'

Two days later Valentino was told that his wife had applied, in Paris, for a divorce. He issued a statement saying he would not contest her action. He intended to defer to his wife's wishes in the matter. 'It is no longer a question of love, but of pride,' he said.

On November 14, as Valentino departed for Britain and the European premiere of *The Eagle* in London, Natacha told reporters that it was still her intention to have a career. If her husband wanted a housewife, he would have to look again. Observers thought she had seriously misjudged her husband's reaction to the threat of divorce, but if she was disappointed at his not rushing to her side and begging for another chance, she was too old a hand in the game of marital fencing to let it show.

TWENTY-FOUR

I dare not fight; but I will wink and hold out my iron.
William Shakespeare (1564–1616)

AS HE BOARDED the *Leviathan* to sail, once more, from America to England, a grim and unsmiling Valentino remembered the similar voyage he had made with Natacha, just two years before, when it seemed that nothing could mar their idyllic existence. 'Now that is all over,' he told reporters who saw him off and noted how sad he appeared.

When he arrived in Britain, on a dull and depressing November day that matched his mood, he switched on his professional brave face: 'Your dull London weather is a welcome change from California's perpetual sunshine,' he said. 'Pleasing as the sun is, you can get a bit weary of him, and London does you good as a change.'

If they believed that, they'd believe anything, and Valentino was eager that the British public should never believe that image of him as a smooth lounge lizard, lying around smoking scented cigarettes and oozing the irresistible attraction of a carefully-nurtured hot-house plant: 'I know,' he told Pressmen, 'that I am thought to be largely an indoor man. But actually I don't suppose anybody lives more out of doors than I do.'

It was a substantial claim, which Rudy was only too willing to back up: 'I have just bought a new home further out of Hollywood—which is becoming slightly

181

overbuilt—and there are five or six acres around it, in which I have arranged a fine big ring. I go for a gallop in it about five o'clock every morning. I keep five horses— one of which is specially trained and pampered for film work. Then I do a good deal of fencing and boxing. Recently I have been learning from Jack Dempsey some of his most effective punches. The learning was slightly dangerous at times, but I survived.'

Action Man needed all his skills-for-survival a few days later when he turned up for the opening of *The Eagle* at the Marble Arch Pavilion. For hours before the premiere, thousands of women and girls had besieged the cinema, struggling with police, haggling with touts (who were asking more than five pounds for tickets) and blocking the entrance to those lucky enough to have been invited.

When Valentino arrived, the severely-tested police could cope no longer. Screaming women broke through the cordon and surrounded the star, grabbing at his coat, his arms, his hair. Those who could not get near shrieked his name again and again in a chilling, monotonous litany. Others, clambering to get a better view, pulled down advertisement boards, whose glass shattered and broke.

With police shoving and pulling hysterical girls from him, Valentino shouldered his way into the cinema, where attendants struggled to close the doors against the surging mass battling to keep them open.

Inside, and safely installed in a box usually reserved for royalty, Valentino was asked to address the audience. 'See if you like the film first,' he said, and they did, cheering and applauding every time he appeared on the screen.

Afterwards, to get to the stage without being mobbed

by the crowds who still surged round every doorway, he reverted to his action man role, following a lamp-carrying attendant up a flight of stairs, across the cinema roof, down an iron ladder, back into the building, down more stairs, though a concrete cellar under the stage ... and eventually into the limelight. The audience went wild as he appeared, immaculate in evening dress, the spotlight flashing on that slave bracelet they'd read about, as he held up his hands for silence.

'My last picture,' he tried to say above the noise, 'was not such a very good one...'

'No, no, Rudy,' they yelled. Middle-aged ladies and smartly-dressed gay young things joined over-excited schoolgirls in the chorus of protest. 'No, no, Rudy!'

'But now,' he added, with ludicrous understatement, 'I think I have won back a place in your hearts...'

It was too much. 'Yes, yes!' screamed the middle-aged, the gay young things, the schoolgirls. 'Oh, yes, Rudy, yes!'

And then he was gone, slipping out of a side door to avoid the mob, many of whom would wait until long after midnight, believing that he wouldn't go without saying goodbye to them, somehow, personally.

As he left, one intrepid reporter stuck close to him to ask a last, though often-posed question: What is your secret? How do you do this to women?

'I don't know,' he said. 'This is a matter-of-fact age, and everyone is starving for romance. I suppose they like me because I bring that romance into their lives for a few moments.'

For a man from whose life the romance had so recently gone, it was a curiously apposite remark.

Shortly afterwards he was in Paris, and the French capital noted that one thing had not been changed by his separation from Natacha. His spending. He entertained in both London and Paris on a lavish scale and the bills forwarded to Ullman in America were enormous, prompting him to speed urgent cables to Valentino advising that he was only again running seriously into debt.

The incident which caused Ullman and the United Artists hierachy most concern, and which sent shivers of dread speeding up their spines, also occurred in Paris. It ended in fiasco, but might easily have robbed his manager and studio of their biggest earner.

Valentino was leaving his hotel one evening when he was confronted by a well-dressed stranger, who introduced himself as the Baron Imre Lukatz, the Hungarian millionaire who had fallen in love with Vilma Banky, and who had threatened to kill the great lover on sight. Faced with the man he had publicly declared to be his arch enemy, the Baron began to scream abuse, and launched a two-fisted attack on the actor. Valentino responded with an uppercut which would have earned praise from his friend Jack Dempsey and deposited the Hungarian on his back. By this time thoroughly roused, Valentino challenged the Baron to a duel, which was accepted.

The Baron specified swords, and after appointing seconds the two men agreed to meet at dawn the following morning in the Bois de Boulogne. Accompanied by his seconds Valentino was first to arrive. The Baron turned up twenty minutes late, minus his sword, and immediately offered his apologies. He had heard, he said, that Valentino's relationship with Miss Banky had been confined to the screen. He recognised him as a man of honour and begged his forgiveness.

Greatly relieved, for he himself had had second thoughts, Valentino shook the Baron warmly by the hand, declared that honour had been satisfied, and walked arm in arm with him to their waiting limousines.

A month later, before the Tribunal of the Seine, with neither party present, the French judges heard Natacha's plea for divorce. In evidence it was stated that for two years Monsieur Guglielmi had failed to provide support for his wife. The three judges deliberated briefly and ordered the decree granted.

The same day, Valentino boarded his favourite trans-Atlantic liner, the *Leviathan*, at Cherbourg and set sail for New York, once again a free man.

TWENTY-FIVE

The ruling passion, be it what it will,
The ruling passion conquers reason still.

Alexander Pope (1688–1744)

WITH HAIR SLIGHTLY thinning at the temples and two disastrous marriages behind him, Rudolph Valentino was still the most eligible man in America. His reputation as the great lover might have been based on celluloid evidence, but there were millions of women throughout the world who would have willingly sacrificed everything for just one hour in his arms.

Of all those women, only a handful had the opportunity to meet him and press their suit in person, and one of these was Pola Negri. Tempestuous, passionate, volcanic, hot-blooded and hot-tempered, she wanted Rudy in a very basic and physical way—and made no secret about her earthy ambitions. 'Once Rudy has experienced my love,' declared the tigerish Polish actress, 'he will forget about all other women. I am ready when he is.'

Valentino read of her boast with amusement—but was certainly not averse to using this means of exorcising the ghost of Natacha. He had ordered George Ullman to get rid of everything in Falcon's Lair that could be associated with his second wife. What better than a much-publicised and lighthearted romance to smooth over any lingering doubts in people's minds that he regretted the departure of Natacha? The fans were demanding a romance. They didn't like to see the great lover they had made without a suitable Venus in his arms.

Pola Negri stalked Valentino with the guile and dedication of a trained seductress. The woman who claimed to have captured the heart of Chaplin, and worn his engagement ring, was this time looking for a more permanent union. Marriage was what she had in mind, and she announced her intention of leading Valentino up the aisle.

The woman chosen as go-between to arrange the first meeting of the Hollywood couple was Marion Davis. On several occasions she invited the pair of them to her home, but each time Pola would telephone and make an excuse for not being there. Fully aware that these tactics were designed to arouse his curiosity Valentino played the game, the humour and tolerance of his younger days now fully restored.

Attempting to bring them face to face became an amusement which half the Hollywood community indulged in, but it was, as predicted, Marion Davis who finally brought them together. Valentino did not take his eyes off Pola as he bent to kiss her hand. She bowed her head in confusion. No director could have wrung a finer performance from either star.

Later Pola said she found him handsome, artless and desperately sincere, though completely lacking the intense sexuality that dominated his screen personality. There was a look of unhappiness in his dark eyes, she said, that appealed more to the maternal than the amorous. His true character, she believed, had come across in *Blood and Sand* when, in the magnificent torero costume, he was rather like a vulnerable child all decked out in fancy dress.

Marion Davis winked at Pola as the couple parted and

187

said teasingly to Valentino: 'You've got your wish. Maybe now you'll stop hounding me.' As she walked away, laughing, she signalled to the orchestra, who struck up a popular tango, *La Comparasita*, and the newly-introduced couple began to dance.

'Call it fatalism,' Pola said afterwards, 'but from our very first meeting I knew this man either had to destroy my life or so irrevocably alter its course that it would never again be the same. I knew it, and waved it away. I had met a man acknowledged to be the world's most desirable man, and I desired him. That was all. The rest was no more than romantic gibberish, probably inspired by the indefinite conclusions of the encounter.'

The next time the couple met was at the Biltmore restaurant. Pola was throwing a dinner party for Michael Arlen and Valentino was hosting a party at a nearby table. The fiery volatile actress tried hard to concentrate on her guests but found it impossible to keep her eyes from straying across to the handsome profile just a few feet away. The Italian appeared not to have noticed her, but suddenly Pola felt a hand on her shoulder and turning, looked up into Rudy's smiling face.

'I'd like you to dance with me,' he said.

For Pola there was no resisting. Almost as though in a trance she glided into his arms and was whirled across the room. Just the sensation of his voice breathing in her ear caused tremors of sensuality to surge through her whole body.

'I must see you alone,' said Valentino. 'Get rid of your guests and I'll take you home.'

Pola simply nodded. There was no question of wanting to avoid the inevitable outcome of this move. That night Pola became, several times over, qualified to discount any rumours that Valentino's two marriages to dominant women had reduced him to near impotency. Sated with love, the naked couple lay on the bed in the master suite at Pola's beautiful Beverly Drive mansion, talking properly to each other for the first time. Their urgent need for each other's bodies, Pola told friends gleefully, meant the things that are normally said before lovemaking had to be said afterwards.

From that moment Pola became Valentino's almost constant companion. He was her escort at all the main parties, balls and premieres, and Pola was a regular guest at Falcon's Lair. Alberto, Valentino's brother, who was staying in Hollywood with his family, was also a guest at the house on Bella Drive, and did not approve of this immoral relationship being conducted so openly in public. But Rudy laughingly explained that he was a single man again, and this was how a single man behaved among the Golden People of Hollywood. The great lover, he said, was simply trying to live up to his reputation.

That reputation was due to be even further enhanced by his next project for United Artists. For Joseph Schenck, underlining his skill as a businessman and his ability to judge the right film vehicle for the star, had purchased the screen rights to Edith Hull's new novel, *The Sons of the Sheik*. One of the twin sons would be eliminated and Valentino, would portray the other.

The film, Ullman predicted jubilantly, would earn for Valentino more than a million dollars. Inspired by this prospect Rudy startled United Artists chiefs by suggesting he play a double role. That of the son, and also of the original sheik, Ahmed Ben Hassan, the part that had first launched him as the most romantic figure in cinema history.

Adding to his excitement was the news that George

Fitzmaurice was at last to direct him in a picture, and Vilma Banky was to be his co-star. Schenck had even secured Agnes Ayres to recreate her portrayal of Diana, the old sheik's wife.

Valentino seemed to blossom with the hardship of filming in the Arizona and Californian deserts. He insisted on absolute realism in the filming of *The Son of the Sheik* and although his fellow actors cursed the severity of sandstorms whipped up by the giant wind machines he persisted in using at full power, they thrilled with him at reports from the studio in Hollywood that rushes were the best and most exciting ever processed.

This premature verdict was more than fully endorsed when the picture was premiered at Grauman's Million Dollar Theatre in Los Angeles. A huge gathering of stars, including the original big four of United Artists and all Valentino's friends, were part of the packed audience which cheered, clapped and stamped their feet in approval and provided him with the greatest ovation ever received by a star on 'home territory'.

Unencumbered by the embarrassing presence of Natacha, Valentino was now a welcome visitor to the most exclusive homes on the West Coast. Pola Negri sometimes irritated with her inevitable talk of marriage but was an amusing, passionate and uncomplicated companion. His friends were now free to come and go in his home as they pleased. Soon he would be a wealthy man. But following completion of *The Son of the Sheik* Valentino became once more moody and unpredictable. Ullman put it down to the constant pestering he received from fans. Douglas Gerrard blamed it on the difficulty Valentino was having sleeping and Schenck claimed it was natural post-production depression which most stars suffered. Whatever the reason, Valentino was not happy and this manifested itself in the way he drove his fast and expensive motor cars.

Soon his reckless driving began to concern his friends, who refused to ride with him if he was driving. Douglas Gerrard accompanied him to San Francisco in his Isotta Fraschini limousine only because Rudy had a chauffeur doing the driving. But on the return trip Valentino took over the wheel after promising Gerrard he would keep to a reasonable speed. Gradually though the speedometer inched higher, and a few miles after San Luis Obispo the big limousine, going at high speed, skidded across the wet highway, careered over some railroad tracks, causing the driver of an approaching Southern Pacific locomotive to slam on his brakes, and struck a telegraph pole. Valentino and Gerrard were uninjured though badly shaken, but the chauffeur and valet were cut and bruised and needed hospital treatment. All four men were rushed to the nearest hospital in a police car and the star was treated for shock.

In need of treatment for shock too were Ullman and Joseph Schenck when they heard the details of the accident. If the hottest box office property in Hollywood could not look after himself, argued Schenck, then he must be taken care of. He summoned the actor to his office and forbade him to make further automobile trips outside the city and never to drive at more than fifty miles an hour.

Had the studio boss witnessed a scene at Pola Negri's Beverly Drive home a few nights later, he would have had far more cause for concern. Sitting with her in her living room, Rudy suddenly became very pale, got up and stumbled through the French windows leading to the garden. Alarmed, the actress hurried after him and found him doubled up with pain on a garden chair.

When she asked what was troubling him he replied: 'It's nothing. It will soon pass. I didn't want you to see me like this. I feel so ashamed of myself.'

Gradually his colour returned and he lit a cigarette, explaining to Pola that he was taking medication because he feared he was going bald, and that this seemed to be harming everything else. With his natural fear of doctors he had not consulted an expert, but was convinced the attacks would cease if he gave up the patent baldness cure.

To cover his embarrassment, Valentino invited Pola to view his new motor yacht and join him on a trip to Catalina. This new toy was seen as great therapy for the actor by his friends. He did everything aboard for himself. Cleaning, polishing—even cooking the meals. In common with most big eaters he was an excellent cook and Ullman once proposed he be awarded the diamond belt at cooking spaghetti.

Valentino also called up June Mathis. Their last meeting had been a harrowing one, for Natacha had accused June of sabotaging *The Hooded Falcon* by delaying production of a suitable script. Rudy met his old friend at a quiet restaurant in Hollywood and they spent several hours together, chatting over his early days as a star and the making of *The Four Horsemen*. This eagerness to see June Mathis again and re-establish their former relationship before leaving for the East to publicise *The Son of the Sheik* suggested a pre-knowledge that it was the last opportunity he would have to heal the rift.

But Valentino seemed to have recovered all his old gaiety, and even joked that June seriously risked having her eyes scratched out by the notoriously jealous Pola through dining with him so intimately.

A week later, in the first days of July, Valentino left

Hollywood by train for New York, intending to change trains in Chicago. As usual a large crowd gathered at the station in Los Angeles to see him off. Among them was Pola Negri. As Valentino himself had done when saying farewell to Natacha at this same station, Pola violated the superstition of watching a loved one out of sight. She stood on the platform waving and shouting after Rudy, who hung from the back of the observation car, ignoring the efforts of the guard to close the door. He waved his hand until a curve in the track carried him from her sight.

It was the last time Pola Negri saw Rudolph Valentino alive.

TWENTY-SIX

A bit of talcum
is always walcum

Ogden Nash (1902–71)

FOR DAYS NOW an oppressive sweltering heat had hung heavily over the cities, leaving the citizenry lethargic, surly, short-tempered—and highly susceptible to the hardy annual silly season story.

And it was just such a story that was about to break, to release waves of laughter, sniggers and innuendo throughout the country, to introduce a new word for effeminacy into the English language, and to haunt Rudolph Valentino for the rest of what was left of his life.

A reporter stumbled across the story when he went to the toilet : the management of a new ballroom had installed in their men's room a slot-machine which dispensed talcum-powder, via pink powder puffs, for those of its customers desirous of odorising themselves for the night of love and lust which lay (hopefully) ahead.

It might, with luck, have been killed on a copy-editor's spike. It might, with judgment, have found its rightful place as an inconsequential down-page paragraph. But Chicago in those days—as the late, great and eminently praiseworthy Ben Hecht (1894–1964) was later to recall with wit and stylish candour—was a frontier town with rich pickings for journalists, and this was one of them too good to lose. The story was seized upon by a *Chicago Tribune* editorial writer, who proceeded to put his tongue in his cheek and humourously protest that Rudolph Valentino was solely responsible for the 'effeminisation' of the All-American Male.

He went to his task, and his typewriter, with unsuppressed glee. 'A new public ballroom was opened on the north-side a few days ago, a truly handsome place and apparently well-run. The pleasant impression lasts until one steps into the men's washroom and finds there, on the wall, a contraption of glass tubes and levers and a slot for the insertion of a coin. The glass tubes contain a fluffy pink solid, and beneath them one reads an amazing legend which runs something like this: 'Insert coin. Hold personal puff beneath the tube. Then pull the lever.'

'A powder vending machine! In a men's washroom!' The writer was by now boggling, wide-eyed and all innocent, over the discovery. 'Homo Americanus!' he protested. 'Why didn't someone quietly drown Rudolph Guglielmi, alias Valentino, years ago?'

'And was the pink powder machine pulled from the wall or ignored? It was not. It was used. We personally saw two "men" step up, insert coin, hold kerchief beneath the spout, pull the lever, then take the pretty pink stuff and put it on their cheeks in front of the mirror.

'Another member of this department, one of the most benevolent men on earth, burst raging into this office the other day because he had seen a young "man" combing his pomaded hair in the elevator. But we claim our pink powder story beats this all hollow.'

What had all this to do with Valentino? The *Tribune* man was coming to that eventually, and somewhat tortuously: 'Is this degeneration into effeminacy a cognate reaction with pacifism to the virilities and realities of the war?' he asked. 'Are pink powder and parlour pinks in any way related? How does one reconcile masculine cosmetics, sheiks, floppy pants and slave bracelets with a disregard for law and an aptitude for crime more in keeping with the frontier of half a century ago than a twentieth-century metropolis?

'It is a strange social phenomenon, and one that is running its course not only here in America but in Europe as well. Chicago may have its powder puffs; London has its dancing men and Paris its gigolos. Down with Decatur; up with Elinor Glyn. Hollywood is the national school of masculinity, Rudy, the beautiful gardener's boy, is the prototype of the American male. Hell's bells. Oh, Sugar.'

The piece brought from the *Tribune*'s readers what the writer intended: a giggle. From Valentino it brought a fury which he allowed to overwhelm him, and which elevated a piece of journalistic jokery to that dangerous area where questions of honour and principle, of manliness and courage, are mouthed and, worse still, meant.

He read the editorial with mounting anger, as he breakfasted at the Blackstone Hotel in Chicago, where he was waiting to change trains on the way from San Francisco to New York.

And the cool, controlled, unflappable lover of the screen exploded in a flow of curses, in English and Italian, that would have stunned his more mature and matronly admirers into shocked silence.

Ullman urged him: 'Forget it. That sort of rubbish is not worth worrying about.'

But Valentino would not be calmed. His pride was hurt. All the publicity work on his image, with those manly, bare-torso beefcake photographs, might count for nothing. He cursed and stormed and threatened. 'Who wrote it?' he demanded of reporters in the hotel. 'I'll go right to his office and show him who's a man.'

Instead, when his rage subsided sufficiently, Valentino decided on another course of defending his honour—and made the massive mistake of issuing a direct challenge, in the form of an open letter 'to the Man (?) who wrote the editorial headed Pink Powder Puffs in Sunday's Tribune'.

In the challenge, (which the *Tribune*'s rival *Chicago Herald-Examiner* was only too happy to publish) Valentino came straight to the point. 'The above-mentioned editorial is at least the second scurrilous attack you have made upon me, my race, and my father's name,' he complained. 'You slur my Italian ancestry; you cast ridicule upon my Italian name; you cast doubt upon my manhood. I call you, in return, a contemptible coward, and to prove which of us is a better man, I challenge you to a personal test.'

Although Alphonse Capone and his associates were currently shooting themselves and Chicago into headlines and history, Rudolph planned to play this one strictly by the rules. 'This is not a challenge to a duel in the generally accepted sense,' he explained. 'That would be illegal. But in Illinois, boxing is legal. So is wrestling. I therefore defy you to meet me in the boxing or wrestling arena to prove, in typically American fashion (for I am an American citizen) which of us is more a man.'

Nor, he emphasised, was this to be a stunt. 'I prefer this test of honour to be private, so that I may give you the beating you deserve, and because I want to make it absolutely plain that this challenge is not for purposes of publicity. I am handing copies of this to the newspapers simply because I doubt that anyone so cowardly as to write about me as you have would respond unless forced by the Press to do so.'

Whom he was so stoutly challenging, he did not care. 'I do not know who you are, or how big you are,' he declared. 'But this challenge stands if you are as big as Jack Dempsey. I will meet you immediately or give you time in which to prepare, for I assume that your muscles must be flabby and weak, judging by your cowardly mentality, and that you will have to replace the vitriol in your veins for red blood—if there be a place in such a body as yours for red blood and manly muscle.'

Having laid those ground rules, he summed up. 'I want to make it plain that I hold no grievance against the *Chicago Tribune*, although it seems a mistake to let a cowardly writer use its valuable columns as this "man" does. My fight is personal—with the poison-pen writer of the editorial that stoops to racial and personal prejudice. The *Tribune*, through Miss Mae Tinee, has treated me and my work kindly, and at times very favourably. I welcome criticism of my work as an actor—but I resent with every muscle of my body attacks upon my manhood and ancestry!'

And in closing: 'Hoping I will have an opportunity to demonstrate to you that the wrist under a slave bracelet may snap a real fist into your sagging jaw, and that I may teach you respect of a man even though he happens to prefer to keep his face clean, I remain, With utter contempt, Rudolph Valentino.

'P.S. I will return to Chicago within ten days. You may send your answer to me in New York, care of United Artists Corp, 729 7th Avenue.'

The challenge was thrown down, and immediately picked up by the Press—notably by the *Tribune*'s powerful rival *Chicago Herald and Examiner*, a William Randolph Hearst production which knew a good story when it wrote one and was so dedicated to the art of winning new readers that it had, a few thousand editions ago, hired the Irish-extracted former choirboy, singing waiter and road-accident victim Dion 'Gimpy' O'Banion as its rough-and-tumble 'circulation manager to prevent the opposition treading on the tender toes and precious pitches of its vendors. (He had, incidentally and alas, ignored his mother's wise advice never to resign, and quit 'the Print' in favour of the currently more popular and profitable bootlegging business—a rash and most regrettable step which, accompanied by some ill-chosen words about his competitors—'To hell with them Sicilians'—ensured his premature demise when six shots were fired all-too accurately in his direction around the lunch-time of Monday, November 10, 1924, in the florists' shop he used as a facade to hide his more nefarious activities.)

The silly season saga grew out of all proportion and Valentino *v*. The Writer became a buzzing, if not a burning, topic of conversation.

Back in New York, Valentino faced several situations which gave him the chance to prove his courage. He accepted them all without question, severely testing the nerve of Ullman who, quite naturally, did not want to see his star charge's health jeopardised unnecessarily.

First Frank O'Neil, the *New York Evening Journal*'s boxing writer, called Ullman wanting to know if Valentino was the athlete his publicity made him out to be. 'Would he,' O'Neil asked, 'agree to a friendly bout between the two of us?'

Ullman hesitated: O'Neil was a big man—and an expert. But Valentino insisted on accepting and, in a brief but well-publicised scrap on the roof of the Ambassador Hotel, had the great satisfaction of sending at least one uppitty gentleman of the Press crashing to his knees on the gravel-surfaced 'ring'.

O'Neil, who'd managed to get a few well-intentioned slaps at the screen's most famed features, was nevertheless well enough to announce to colleagues after the fight: 'That boy has a punch like the kick of a mule. I'd sure hate to have him sore at me.'

Valentino was delighted at the success of his public demonstration of the manly art. He liked and admired boxers, and some of them were his friends.

He would, incidentally, have been proud to know that, down in Louisville, Kentucky, he had a future fan in Odessa Lee O'Grady who would give birth to one of the world's greatest boxers. When her first son weighed into the world, at 6lb 7oz on January 17, 1942, Odessa would name the pretty little boy after his father, who himself was named after a former American Ambassador to the Court of St. James's, an unsuccessful Vice-Presidential candidate and leading Southern abolitionist—Cassius Marcellus Clay. Her second son she would name Rudolph Valentino Clay.

*   *   *

A few days later, after seeing brother Alberto off to Paris aboard the *France*, Valentino turned up for the New York premiere of *The Son of the Sheik* at the Mark Strand Theatre—and walked into more trouble. All day crowds had been gathering, waiting in the stifling, hot streets to catch a glimpse of the film's hero, and police chiefs, fearing trouble, ordered a mounted patrol to the theatre to control the crowds. They cleared a path for Valentino to get into the theatre, where he made a short speech to an audience of sighing, adoring fans.

Getting out afterwards was not going to be so easy.

Thousands of women lay in wait outside, every one of them eager to get their hands on the man. Ullman, fearing for Valentino's well-being for the second time in a few days, whispered to him: 'Follow me,' and Rudy knew the drill. Suddenly Ullman, with Valentino's hands on his shoulders, head-charged the crowd, running in roughly the direction of their waiting car. As they ran, Valentino heard the sound of buttons being ripped from his coat, felt hands reach out to grab his pocket handkerchief, others snatching the hat from his head, and even the cuff-links from his shirt. The car's motor was running as they reached it and slammed the door, only partly shutting out the hysterical, agonised screams of women who'd been so close and yet so far from the man they idolised.

In comparative safety, Rudy turned to Ullman. 'We made it,' he smiled.

Ullman wiped his brow. 'Only just,' he said.

Then, as the limousine began to pull away, with a police escort, to their horror they saw a woman jump from the crowd and hurl herself on to the running board. Equally as quickly, she was dragged back by the mob and fell to the pavement with a sickening thud that could be clearly heard above the screams. 'Stop, for God's sake stop!' Valentino screamed at the chauffeur. It was too late: the woman had disappeared into the crowd, how badly hurt they could not know. Back at his hotel, Valentino immediately insisted on telephoning the local police stations. Had there been any reports of a woman hurt in an auto accident? he asked. 'Nope, nothing reported,' he was told.

Relieved, and needing to relax after a hectic day, Valentino called up Jean Acker and suggested that they and a few friends hit the town.

He knew exactly the place to hit: Texas Guinan's, a hot, crowded, lavishly-furnished speakeasy run by the personable former actress Mary Louise Cecilia 'Tex' Guinan, to which film and theatre stars, politicians and millionaires flocked for wild parties and striptease shows and the honour of paying absurd prices for 'champagne', which tasted strangely like zizzed-up soda water.

You could get a genuine bottle of whisky for not much over one hundred dollars, and Texas, who was frequently raided by police and those damn sneaky prohibition agents, thought it good value. 'There's a lot of talk,' she explained, 'about how I take the customers for all they've got. It's not as bad as that—even if there aren't any charity wards in my club. The boys come here to spend, and I'm not going to disappoint them. When they drink ginger ale in my place, they are drinking liquid platinum, and they like it.'

It was *the* place for the gregarious and generous, free-spending Valentino to be seen, and before they could contribute funds towards Tex's future happiness, Valentino and Jean were seen by reporters with the inevitable question: 'Is there a possibility that you two might get round to remarrying?'

Jean smiled through closed lips. Valentino gave the inevitable reply: 'We are good friends, and always will be.' It was enough to make the gossip columns next day.

Inside, Tex Guinan bounded up to Valentino's party. 'Great to see you. Can I introduce Rahmin Bey?'

The Indian fakir, currently amazing audiences with his feats of magic, bowed low and addressed Valentino. 'Would you care,' he asked, 'to help me with a little experiment?'

Rudy shrugged. 'Sure, what is it?'

'With your permission,' smiled the mystic, 'I will

thrust a needle through your cheek—without pain, and without drawing blood.'

Valentino agreed—it might help spread the word that he was frightened of no man, or physical test. But George Ullman, who in the past few days had seen his asset only too willingly expose himelf to danger, brawling in public and being mobbed by over-eager fans, put his foot down at this little exercise. 'Don't be crazy,' he told Valentino. 'There just could be an accident. You can't do it.'

By now, all eyes were on the star. The audience were expecting something sensational, and Valentino was not going to disappoint them. He agreed that the needle should be put through his arm, stood up, stripped off his coat and rolled up his shirtsleeves. Then, with the room hushed and expectant, and Ullman looking on with mounting anxiety, Valentino watched in fascination as the magician thrust the long needle through his forearm—and withdrew it, without drawing blood and without pain.

The audience gasped and broke into applause. Valentino smiled, rolled down his shirtsleeve and pulled on his coat. And Ullman, fussing like a mother-hen that the needle might not be clean and fearing an infection, called a waiter to bring alcohol to clean the experimental area.

With prices like Tex's, it was highly expensive preventative medicine.

*   *   *

The next few days were spent having a good time—most of it with Jean Acker—but the Powder Puff Affair was his main preoccupation. He mentioned it increasingly, to Jean, to Ullman, to friends. He could not wait to get back to Chicago, and when he did, the reporters' questions were predictable. 'Have you received a reply to your challenge?' 'Who is your opponent?' 'When will the confrontation be?' He answered them all with a statement which brought the farce crashing down in anti-climax.

'It is evident you cannot make a coward fight, any more than you can draw blood from a turnip,' he said. And added, with heavy sarcasm: 'The heroic silence of the writer who chose to attack me without provocation in the *Chicago Tribune* leaves no doubt as to the total absence of manliness in his whole make-up. I feel I have been vindicated because I consider his silence as a tacit retraction and an admission I am forced to accept, even though it is not entirely to my liking.'

Still playing fair, he added a tribute. 'The newspaper men and women whom it has been my privilege to know briefly, or for a long time, have been absolutely fair, and so loyal to their profession and their publications that I need hardly say how conspicuous is this exception to the newspaper profession.'

And that, it seemed, was that. It should have been. But the whole ludicrous affair would not lie down. It preyed on his mind and continued to worry him. The insult did not lose its sting, and Valentino kept wondering if he'd played the whole scenario properly or if, by issuing his challenge, he had become the only possible loser by bringing himself into more ridicule. If only, he thought, he had gone earlier for advice to one of those journalists he had known only briefly.

The journalist, Henry Louis Mencken—already a legend among newspapermen—was puzzled when he was told Valentino wanted to see him. They had never met before. He had never written about him or even seen one of his films. But Valentino, reading a piece by Mencken, had judged him a shrewd observer, and wanted his advice on the problem that was bedevilling him. Mencken was pleased to oblige.

They met, in a New York hotel, as the heatwave continued, and Mencken's first impression of the star, when they both took off their jackets, was how absurd Valentino's extraordinarily thick, wide braces looked on such a slim young man—especially on a hot summer night.

For an hour they suffered the heat, mopping their faces with their handkerchiefs, the napkins, the corners of the tablecloth, and towels brought by a waiter. Then a thunderstorm broke, they began to breathe—and Valentino poured out his troubles. Mencken listened patiently, but could offer no consolation. The damage, he said, had been done. Valentino should have shrugged off the Chicago journalist's jibe with a lofty snort—or perhaps better still, a counter-jibe. He should have stayed away from the reporters. But now he was insulted and ridiculed and there was nothing he could do about it, and he should let the affair die a natural death.

'That's infamous,' Valentino protested.

'Nothing,' Mencken replied, 'is infamous that is not true. A man still has his inner integrity.'

They talked and sweated and seemed to get nowhere. Then, Mencken recalled, in what was probably the most shrewd assessment ever made of Valentino's character, 'suddenly it dawned upon me—I was too dull or it was too hot for me to see it sooner—that what we were talking about was really not what we were talking about at all. I began to observe Valentino more closley. A curiously naïve and boyish young fellow, certainly not much beyond thirty and with a disarming air of inexperience. To my eye, at least, not handsome, but nevertheless, rather attractive.

'There was some obvious fineness in him; even his

205

clothes were not precisely those of his horrible trade. He began by talking of his home, his people, his early youth. His words were simple and yet somehow very eloquent. I could still see the mime before me, but now and then, briefly and darkly, there was a flash of something else. That something else, I concluded, was what is commonly called, for want of a better name, a gentleman. In brief, Valentino's agony was the agony of a man of relatively civilised feelings thrown into a situation of intolerable vulgarity, destructive alike to his peace and to his dignity—nay, into a whole series of such situations.

'It was not that trifling Chicago episode that was riding him; it was the whole grotesque futility of his life. Had he achieved, out of nothing, a vast and dizzy success? Then that success was hollow as well as vast—a colossal and preposterous nothing. Was he acclaimed by yelling multitudes? Then every time the multitudes yelled, he felt himself blushing inside.

'The old story of Diego Valdez once more, but with a new poignancy in it. Valdez, at all events, was High Admiral of Spain. But Valentino, with his touch of fineness in him—he had his commonness, too, but there was that touch of fineness—Valentino was only the hero of the rabble.'

At first, Mencken judged, Valentino's situation must have only bewildered him. But now it was revolting him—and worse, making him afraid : 'Here was a young man who was living daily the dream of millions of other young men. Here was one who was catnip to women. Here was one who had wealth and fame.

'And here was one who was very unhappy.'

TWENTY-SEVEN

Across the wires the electric message came:
'He is no better, he is much the same.'
Attributed to Alfred Austin (1835–1913)

IF HE WAS desperately unhappy, Rudolph Valentino was certainly not showing it. Back in New York, and thrilled with the success of the Chicago premiere of *The Son of the Sheik*, he hurled himself into a gruelling round of parties and enjoyment. 'I'm having the time of my life,' he told Ullman, as he turned night into day and played those days away.

Duty, in the form of promoting the new picture, occasionally called, and he travelled to Atlantic City to attend a showing of it at the Virginia Theatre. Afterwards, as a favour, he made another personal appearance at the Ritz-Carlton revue run by his old friend Gus Edwards, who presented him with a pair of boxing gloves. They might, Edwards suggested, be needed to thrash that *Chicago Tribune* writer.

Smiling, Valentino accepted the gift, but declined an invitation to dance with a girl from the revue. Edwards insisted, and eventually he agreed. But as the music began, and Valentino swept the girl across the stage, neither he, nor she, nor the audience, could know that this was his last tango.

After another *Son of the Sheik* opening, in Brooklyn, he had time free until August 16, when he was due to do another personal appearance in Philadelphia, and he filled the days with fun and the nights with friends. He called up Adolph Zukor and, over a friendly lunch, told him: 'I'm sorry about the studio trouble I made.'

Zukor shrugged: 'Forget it. In this business, if we can't disagree and then forget about it, we'll never get anywhere.' And then he added the words he would never be able to forget: 'You're young. Many good years are ahead of you.'

There was, then, no reason to think otherwise. Shortly before, a doctor had passed Valentino as perfectly healthy, and only hermits and nuns of enclosed orders had not seen at least one photograph of him at his keep-fit exercises. ('How beautiful! How strong!' oozed the caption-writer of Hearst's *New York Daily Mirror*—a close copy of its British namesake—under one picture of the bare-bodied star, flexing his muscles all over page one.)

For some time, though, he had suffered stomach pains, often acute, and friends had urged him to at least mention them to a doctor. 'Indigestion,' he said, and kept on taking only bicarbonate of soda to ease the pain while he continued eating his beloved Italian dishes, chain-smoking, and living life to the full. Constantly, Ullman begged him to ease up, to relax more, sleep more. Valentino, as though bent on wringing the last minutes of pleasure from his free time, ignored him. The parties went on, and the pace began to tell.

One night—and George Ullman would always remember that Saturday night of August 14, 1926—Valentino prepared for another party. Ullman noticed that the colour in his face had changed. 'Come home early,' he suggested, 'and get some rest.' Another session of personal appearances, he reminded him, were starting next week.

Valentino looked up, eyes ablaze. 'Rest?' he laughed. 'Why, I feel wonderful. I don't need rest.' And left for the party.

It was held, in his honour, at the apartment of one Barclay Warburton Jnr., and attended by some sixteen people. It began around 10 pm, lasted until the early hours and was the last Rudolph Valentino would ever attend. Next day, shortly before noon, he collapsed in his room at the Ambassador Hotel, and Ullman found him there clutching his stomach, writhing and moaning in agony.

He called doctors, who said that Valentino must be rushed to New York's Polyclinic Hospital immediately. There, at 6 pm the same evening, he was operated on for acute appendicitis and a gastric ulcer. By 7 pm the operation was over, and shortly after 10 pm, when the effects of the anaesthetic had worn off, the patient opened his eyes and asked a doctor: 'Well, then, did I behave like a pink powder puff or like a man?'

The operation appeared, at first, to have been a success, and doctors said the ulcerous condition was more of a menace to his health than the appendicitis. During the next few days the VIP patient, appearing to be on the mend, slept most of the time and was allowed visits from only Ullman.

Sitting up in bed, wearing white silk pyjamas, he told his manager: 'No, don't send for my brother. Just cable him and say I'm a little indisposed and will soon be all right. And wire Pola the same.' When Ullman said he wished it was he who was in the hospital bed, Valentino protested: 'Don't be silly. You have little children and family responsibilities, whereas I...' His voice trailed off and he turned his face away.

Later he asked for a mirror, and Ullman, not wanting him to see the tired, white face of an ill man, asked why. 'I just want to see what I look like when I'm sick,' said Valentino, 'so that if I ever have to play the part in pictures, I'll know how to put on the right make-up.'

He was thinking again of his films, and his fans, and they were constantly thinking of him. From the time the news of his illness broke, crowds of women had waited at the hospital, hoping to see or just hear of their idol. An armed guard was put at his door, in case the more hysterical of them tried to rush in to his bedside. There was little hope of that: even close friends were not allowed near and Jean Acker, distressed that she was refused permission to see him, had to send in instead a coverlet and pillows, with his name embroidered on them.

Cables and telegrams poured in from all parts of America and the world, and a special secretary was hired to look after them. Bouquet after bouquet of flowers arrived, along with other gifts, and health cures, and Bibles and words of advice and prayers and lots and lots of love and deep concern.

The patient, meanwhile, appeared to be making good progress. By the Thursday he was reported 'in good spirits' and doctors, noting his courage and 'remarkable constitution', were confident that his recovery would be complete. His fans outside were not so certain. When a rumour that he had died swept like wildfire through the country, thousands telephoned the hospital and extra staff were drafted to the switchboard.

'*Is it true,*' *the callers hardly dared ask,* '*about Rudy ...?*'

'Mr. Valentino,' intoned the operators, 'is alive and his condition is the same.'

'Thank God, and thank you...'

By Saturday, he was thinking about getting out of hospital. When he woke up at seven o'clock that morning, he told Ullman: 'I feel fine now. The pain is all gone and I can feel the place where they made the incision. By Monday I can have friends in, and by Wednesday I can go back to the hotel—taking the nurses, of course.'

That, his own bulletin on his condition, more than worried the doctors who had held out high hopes for him. They made yet another thorough examination and consulted together for almost an hour. Their verdict: the cessation of pain Valentino had talked about was an exceedingly bad sign. Pleurisy had brought about a relapse, and had been followed by septoendocarditis—a poisoning of the wall of the heart.

The doctors considered every possibility open to them, including a blood transfusion. Edward Day, a hospital engineer, volunteered to give a pint of his blood, but it was decided that Valentino was too weak to be able to take the extra strain on his heart.

By early on Sunday morning his fever had increased and his pulse was more rapid. Ullman, realising that he might want a confessor, called Father Leonard, a priest who had come often to the hospital to ask about Valentino, and left him alone in the sickroom with the stricken star. Joseph Schenck and his wife Norma Talmadge, also contacted by Ullman, arrived at the bedside in the early evening, and later Frank Mennillo, an old Italian friend, talked to Valentino. 'Don't worry, Frank,' the actor whispered to him. 'I'm going to be well soon.'

After a quiet night, Valentino woke in great pain at four o'clock on Monday morning and was given a morphine injection to ease his suffering. Even then, he was convinced he would soon be fully recovered. Cheerfully, he asked Dr. Howard D. Meeker: 'Do you know the greatest thing I am looking forward to?'

The doctor asked: 'What is it?'

Valentino told him: 'The fishing review next month. I hope you have plenty of rods.'

He became irrational, talking mainly in Italian, but around 6 am he recognised Ullman by his bedside and called him by his name, in a voice so much stronger than before, that, for a moment, there was fresh hope. Then Valentino spoke again, in a rambling, irrational way, and the hope faded. 'Wasn't it an awful thing that we were lost in the woods last night?' he asked. Ullman, unable to speak, smiled and stroked his hair.

'On the one hand,' Valentino continued, 'you don't appreciate the humour of that.'

'Sure I do Rudy, sure I do,' murmured Ullman.

'On the other hand,' said Valentino, 'you don't seem to appreciate the seriousness of it, either . . .'

The sun was rising. Ullman walked to the window to pull down the blind, but Valentino waved a hand and protested: 'Don't pull down the blinds. I want the sunlight to greet me.'

By 8 am he had lapsed into a coma, opening his eyes occasionally when his name was called. By 10 am Father Joseph Congedo, a priest from Valentino's hometown, had administered the Last Rites of the Holy Roman Catholic Church. By 11 am, news of the star's critical condition had spread and the country, the *Los Angeles Record* reported, was 'waiting each word from his sickroom almost as it waits for a word from the sickroom of a President.' Crowds of men, women and children, including many Italians, gathered outside the hospital, waiting quietly, praying for a miracle they knew now would never come. Police, watching the crowds growing bigger, were forced to move them on.

One last, desperate hope disappeared when a racing plane, flying from Detroit with a special antiseptic preparation for Valentino, had to make a forced landing because of fog before it reached New York. Time was running out, and calls to the hospital switchboard were pouring in by the thousand. All morning the question was the same. All morning the reply was a terse: 'Critical ... condition unchanged.'

Then, shortly before noon, with Valentino's temperature at 105, his pulse hammering 140 strokes to the minute and his respiration at 30 to the minute, an official bulletin declared him 'rapidly failing'. Soon afterwards, at 12.10 pm, on Monday August 23, 1926, 'with a priest's crucifix pressed to his lips', Rudolph Valentino died 'without pain'.

At 12.15 p.m. Joseph Schenck walked slowly down the hospital stairs and read out a brief bulletin signed by three doctors. Rudolph Valentino was dead, at the age of thirty-one, of septic pneumonia and septic endocarditis.

Immediately, the constant flow of calls to the hospital switchboard increased in volume. Now, instead of the clipped, terse, official statement of the patient's condition, the callers heard the news they dreaded delivered by girls who had joined them in their anguish.

'Oh, he's dead ... Rudy's dead.'

TWENTY-EIGHT

Ha! Dead! Impossible! It cannot be
I'd not believe it though himself should swear it
Henry Carey (1693?–1743)

DISBELIEF, A TOTAL shocked incomprehension that he could be dead at such an age, after all those keep-fit pictures and an apparently successful operation, was a general reaction—and a reaction which, almost inevitably, was to bring rumours that he died from something more serious than a stomach complaint.

The first people to hear the news, those who had kept vigil outside the Polyclinic Hospital, took in the awful fact more readily than others would do and, because of their immediacy, reacted much more violently. Within minutes of the announcement, women outside the hospital wept bitterly and screamed hysterically and tore their hair in grief. Some, overcome with emotion, slumped unconscious to the pavement. Others, fainting in the crowd still pressed around the hospital, were stretched out where they lay. Ambulance staff were fetched to carry them away, and police waded in to break up the mounting, mourning, mob.

As the news was flashed around the world, and pre-written obituaries were hurriedly updated to make massive morbid headlines, the life of Valentino was already beginning to become legend. In cities throughout America women fought their way to news-stands, snatched copies of the early editions and, after a few seconds reading, broke down and wept openly.

Their despair was soon shared by millions as the news reached the capitals, the cities, the towns, of the world, and for many of those millions the death of Valentino brought a real and personal grief. For years they would remember vividly exactly where they were, and who they were with, and what time it was when they heard that he was dead.

*   *   *

When Natacha Rambova heard the news she was in Paris, and read it in a cable from George Ullman. When Jean Acker heard the news she was in New York and wept: 'He is gone. What good is it to talk now?' When Alberto heard the news he was in Italy, and made immediate plans to get to America for his brother's funeral. When Edith Maud Winstanley heard the news she was in Derbyshire, and was saddened that the man who had brought her work to a wider audience than she could ever reach was dead.

*   *   *

When Peggy Scott heard the news, she was inconsolable. The pretty and petite young actress wept all day, constantly running her fingers through her bobbed fair hair, crying until her blue eyes were etched with red, repeating his name in whispers again and again.

Depressed, despairing and alone, and surrounded by large photographs of Rudolph Valentino, she sat in a flat at 52 James Street, near London's Oxford Street, and wrote a letter which was to be headlined throughout the world.

'There is a lot,' she said, 'that I cannot tell you. No

one will ever know that with his death my last bit of courage has flown ... I feel that I have been stretched for years, like a piece of elastic. In 1922, Rudolph helped me to carry on. He told me a lot of his own sufferings, and perhaps it was only a matter of time before the elastic snapped. Please look after Rudolph's pictures. He has helped me over lots of stiles unknowingly.'

She re-read the letter, fingering the single row of pearls at her neck, and then, at the age of twenty-seven, took her own life by poison—a death draught of mercuric chloride, more commonly called corrosive sublimate.

When police arrived, they were confronted with a mystery: just who was Peggy Scott? And how well did she know Valentino? They learned that, in recent weeks, she had stayed at various houses in and around Baker Street, and had talked freely to local people. Her real name was Mrs. Margaret Murray Scott and, she'd said, she had married at eighteen and was now a widow.

But what really intrigued the police—and the public when they read of the tragedy—was her 'friendship' with Rudolph Valentino. She had told people she met him on a yacht trip to the Mediterranean in 1921, and had danced with him at Biarritz, in the south of France.

On the day he died, she dressed stylishly—fawn coat and skirt, brown felt hat, brown strapped shoes with patent fronts—and suddenly left the room just off Baker Street where she had stayed for the past week. She collected together her luggage—a large suitcase and three attache-cases, hat-box and golf-clubs—changed a pound note to tip the man who carried it downstairs, and then drove off in a taxi, apparently to the flat where she was found dead next day.

And that was all. Police appealed for relatives to contact them. They received several letters about 'Miss Scott' and made inquiries in Norfolk, Norwich and Swindon. But when the inquest was held at Marylebone coroner's court, they had to admit they had discovered nothing about her past.

The Valentino link? It was impossible for her to have met him in the Mediterranean in 1921, the inquest was told, because he was then filming in Hollywood. And letters showed that, at the time she was supposed to be dancing with him in Biarritz, she was, in fact, in Rome.

'One has not definitely associated her with Rudolph Valentino,' said the coroner, and recorded a verdict of Suicide during Temporary Insanity.

There was a lot of it around at the time.

*　　　*　　　*

When Charles Chaplin heard the news, he said: 'The death of Rudolph Valentino is one of the greatest tragedies that has occurred in the history of the motion picture industry. As an actor he attained fame and distinction; as a friend he commanded love and admiration. We of the film industry, through his death, lose a very dear friend, a man of great charm and kindliness.'

When Rosalind and Cecily Crawford, aged fourteen and fifteen, heard the news they were in London and 'cried and cried for ages' and took to wearing black armbands. Only last year the sisters, deeply devoted to Valentino, had sat for seven hours, and repeated showings of *The Eagle*, at the Marble Arch Cinema until he had appeared on stage. And now they felt as though they never wanted to see another picture ever again ... 'Everything,' they said 'seems so empty.'

When Cecil B. de Mille heard the news, he said: 'In Mr. Valentino's death we have lost a great artist. But, fortunately, we can look on death as progress and not as the finish.'

When Rita and Ada Maldarizzi heard the news they were at home in Castellaneta and wept, remembering the visit their childhood friend had paid them, when they had known, somehow, it was the last time they would see him. They prayed for the repose of his immortal soul.

*　　*　　*

When Pola Negri heard the news she was in her Ambassador Hotel bungalow in Hollywood, where she had been working night and day to finish the film *Hotel Imperial* so that she could rush to Valentino's bedside. Studio officials had sent messengers to her bungalow to break the news as gently as possible.

They were too late. Newsmen had already reached the star and informed her of Valentino's death. She immediately fainted. Her maid, frantically crying for help, summoned a hotel doctor, who brought Miss Negri back to consciousness. Then, completely unnerved, she began to weep and wail bitterly. A few moments later her grief became hysteria and, in a dialect of mixed Polish and English, she began to scream his name again and again: 'Rudy, Rudy. Oh, Rudy!'

Again the doctor, now joined by her personal physician, managed to quieten her, and a woman friend stayed to comfort her. 'The star's hysterical condition,' newsmen reported, 'prevented her from issuing any statement,' but all work on her film was abandoned, and it was assumed that she would leave as soon as she was well enough for New York. Assumed? You could bet your last dollar on it.

*   *   *

When the rest of Hollywood heard the news, it came to a standstill. Flags were lowered to half-mast, directors shouted 'Cut!' and called off work for the day, and actors hurried to executive offices to ask if they knew anything more than that first bare announcement. Women stars wept dramatically and the men tried just as dramatically to put on brave, unflinching faces.

Only at United Artists, the gossip had it, was work even more feverish than usual as laboratory staff put in overtime producing extra prints of *The Son of the Sheik*. Even though its star was dead, he could still appear, and make money, in the cinemas. And now he would be more in demand than ever.

TWENTY-NINE

Anything awful makes me laugh
I misbehaved once at a funeral

Charles Lamb (1775–1834)

MOURNING for Rudolph Valentino did not merely occur, quietly, respectfully, decently and privately. It broke out like some wild contagious disease and, fanned by interested parties stage-managing positively his last—though unfortunately not live—public appearance, brought about one of the most bizarre public farewells in history and mob scenes that New York police described as the worst in the city's records.

Had he known what havoc he was to wreak, Valentino would never have asked his manager to agree to any public request for his body to lie in state. But he did and, complying with that wish, Ullman arranged for Valentino to be moved to Frank E. Campbell's Broadway funeral chapel later on the afternoon of his death. There, morticians worked through the night, scientifically embalming the body, making up the face until it resembled a wax dummy (which some suspicious mourners swore it was), dressing it in full evening clothes and laying it to rest in a bronze coffin, with the face and shoulders exposed to public view.

Even as they worked, crowds began to gather outside, and by the early afternoon of the next day, as a Valentino secretary issued a statement, thanking the 10,000 people who had sent messages of sympathy, thousands of personal mourners were creating havoc outside the funeral parlour. More than 12,000 of them—celebrities, shop-girls, clerks, fashionably-dressed women, youths apeing the Valentino look with their slicked-down hair—blocked every street around the chapel, waiting and watching as florists delivered massive bouquets from the star's friends and little bunches of field-flowers arrived from his fans.

And then it began to rain. A gentle rain—'from Heaven', more than one observed—became a sudden downpour, and police lost all control as the vast crowd began to struggle to reach whatever shelter they could find. Tough, experienced and pathetically-few New York cops swore and cursed, bullied and threatened as the mob surged towards the place where their idol lay. As they did so, the pressure on the chapel's large plate-glass window proved too much and it shattered into thousands of pieces, raining down on screaming, panicking women and girls.

From then on, it could only get worse. Mounted police were forced to make repeated charges into the crowd to try to restore some sort of order. In a mad scramble, one woman was trampled under the hoofs of a police horse and pulled, moaning, from the fray. Scores more were bruised and injured or cut by the flying glass. Others fainted and were carried along by the crowd. Children were torn away from their parents. Police battled to get those hurt to a room in the mortuary which had been turned into an emergency hospital.

When the funeral parlour doors opened, it could only get *much* worse. The mob, knowing now that their patience was about to be rewarded, surged towards the door, sweeping aside police and anyone and anything else that stood between them and the laid-out Latin. They battled, shouting, screaming and swearing, into the Gold Room, where Valentino's body lay, amid an aroma of incense and scented candles, wreaths, bouquets and golden drapes. 'As unreasonably as marching ants', one reporter said in his dispatch from the improbable battle-front, 'the crowds pressed forward in a manner which hurriedly-summoned extra police were entirely unable to block.'

But they were not to stay long. It soon became clear that if drastic action were not taken, and quickly, the room would be completely wrecked by those wishing to pay their 'respects'. The doors were closed, and the coffin moved to a smaller room on the second floor with emergency exits through which people could be hurried back into the streets. Those streets were now littered with torn clothing, broken straw hats, shoes wrenched from feet in the scrambles and, here and there, bars of soap which the more malicious had rubbed on the pavements to bring down the police horses.

When the doors were reopened, it looked for a while as though some sort of order reigned. People were rushed upstairs, rushed past the body—skilfully lit and behind protective glass—and rushed back downstairs and out again. 'Come on, step lively!' ordered police and attendants as men, women and children, some weeping, some merely staring curiously, others giggling, were hurried through.

Those who tried to snatch souvenirs in the room, or step forward to kiss the glass casing, were hustled away with little delicacy. A two-second glance was all they were allowed. Those who appeared to collapse in tears or fall into a faint were just as quickly carted off in the direction of doctors, who said that few were genuine cases of uncontrollable grief: one girl wearing a tragic, tear-stained expression was found to have an onion tucked conveniently into her handkerchief. But then even doctors were not above suspicion. A 'Dr' Sterling C. Wyman, who had been appointed chief physician to help the injured, was later unmasked as an ex-con man cashing in on the proceedings.

Outside, another store window had crashed in splinters. The crowd, now swelled to a guess-estimated 20,000 or more by people who had finished work for the day, was becoming impatient. More women had fainted, more people had been hurt, more police had been called, bringing their strength to around 151—the one being Police Commissioner 'Mac' McLaughlin, who'd decided it was about time he got along to see for himself what the hell was going on down there.

He soon found out, and ordered the doors of the chapel to be closed once more until order prevailed. It was not easy, but by some major miracle of planning and persuasion, police eventually organised a queue and, from 7.30 p.m. until midnight, when the doors were closed for the night, up to 40,000 had glimpsed Valentino for the last time.

Among the last to arrive were a group of men who brought the biggest surprise of the surprise-packed day. As police dispersed the lingering thousands from the area and workmen erected wooden barricades to protect the chapel's windows, the black-shirted men told officials they were from the Fascisti League of America and brought a wreath from no less than Benito Mussolini, who wanted them to mount a guard of honour around their fallen compatriot. The impressed executives of Mr. Frank B. Campbell's emporium were only too glad to welcome them. When a man like Mussolini dictated his wishes, they agreed, it was best to comply.

It rained again next day. The heavens, they said again, were weeping for Rudy. But from early morning, thousands more turned up to view the body, and this time the police were ready for them. They ordered the dripping mourners into a controllable, organised queue, and from 9 a.m. allowed them in to see the coffin, which had been moved to a ground-floor room to speed-up the passage of people through the building. Among them, reporters noticed Mrs. Richard Whittemore, alias 'Tiger Lil', whose husband, a bandit-gang leader known as The Candy Kid, had been hanged only recently in Baltimore. 'Lil', not averse to posing for Press photographs, explained that she had met Valentino at a party some years ago and was here to pay her respects.

The photographers were busy again in the early afternoon when Jean Acker, with members of her family, arrived. Other people were cleared from the room while she said a private farewell to her former husband. Later, between sobs, she was able to say: 'He was the most wonderful man I have ever known.' She had always loved him, she swore. They had remained the best of friends and saw each other frequently. But, no, they had never discussed remarrying. Near to collapse, she was escorted away.

More drama came later in the day when militant anti-Fascists confronted the black-shirted guard of honour, accusing them of offending the name of Valentino, who was, they said, an all-American anti-Fascist himself. The Italian Government, they claimed, knew nothing about a wreath from Mussolini, and had not ordered the guard to be posted. On investigation, the embarrassing truth was discovered: a funeral parlour press agent had hired the Fascisti to lend 'dignity' to the proceedings. George Ullman, horrified at the disclosure and by the morbid, sordid, goings-on, turned up late in the evening and announced that he would tolerate no more of it. Reversing a decision to allow the body to remain on view until Saturday evening, he said it would be removed at midnight to a vault, where it could be seen by only genuine, private mourners. Behaviour at the bier appalled him. 'It is sordid, disgusting, irreverent and morbid,' he said as the last of the day's estimated 50,000 visitors waited to gain admittance.

As New Yorkers caught their last glimpse of Rudy's corpse, British people were catching their first: readers of the one-penny *Daily Sketch* were treated to a picture of Valentino's body lying beneath a Page One headline which boasted: VALENTINO LYING IN STATE: By Wireless. Below it, a caption explained: 'This exclusive picture of Rudolph Valentino lying in state was transmitted by wireless from New York to London in less than an hour. It is reproduced [it added, half-apologising for the poor quality] just as it was received. By arrangement with the Radio Corporation of America and the Marconi Telegraph Company in London, special operators were retained in New York and London to expedite the transmission of the photograph.'

Meanwhile, the subject of this super-scoop was moved once again to the Gold Room where, despite crowds still besieging the building, he was to lie in comparative peace until his funeral the following Monday.

But if wagging tongues could reach and wake the dead, Rudolph Valentino would by now be sitting bolt upright, listening in fascination and horror. From the very moment he died, rumours about his sudden demise had been spawned, spread and embroidered and widely believed by those who could not accept the fact that a gastric ulcer and its complications could snatch away one so young and apparently healthy.

They said he had been shot or stabbed by a jealous rival, poisoned by a spurned woman, coldly done to death by arsenic. Only foul play, the theory went, could be responsible for such a sudden departure.

The shooting rumours began with the mention on the death certificate of perforations. Bullet-holes obviously, the suspicious nodded knowingly. But they were up against the poison rumour-mongers, who claimed that only arsenic could be responsible for the violent pains which caused Valentino to be rushed to hospital in the first place. Their case was backed by a Brooklyn lung specialist who said that if Valentino's face had changed after death, as had been suggested, poisoning could be the cause. 'Septic poisoning alone could not do that,' he declared, and passed on his opinions to Assistant District Attorney Ferdinand Pecora, with a request for an autopsy.

The rumours gained ground when mystery developed about where Valentino had spent his last night. Ziegfeld Follies beauty Marion Kay Benda claimed that she and Rudolph, who were deeply in love, had spent the early part of that Saturday evening at two clubs, including Tex Guinan's, where he had become violently ill. Another version had it that he had spent all the evening at the party, from which he had been rushed directly to the hospital by ambulance at 8.30 a.m.

All that was knocked down by the junior Mr. Warburton, who said there had been no party at his home—and was then himself rushing into hospital for a mysterious operation. Had the poisoner struck again? To try to end the rumours, Dr. Meeker and his assistant doctors issued a statement repeating their original diagnosis of the cause of death. Valentino, said Meeker, 'simply had not taken good care of himself. He must have had a chronic stomach disorder—there were holes in the lining of his stomach as big as your finger.'

Holes? Those bullet-holes again, obviously. Or probably stab wounds. The rumours went on and on. He had been found in a gutter. Jack de Salles' friends had taken their revenge. He had been discovered in the arms of a lover and gunned down by her enraged husband. Everyone, it seemed, had a pet theory that they would not give up. Even a year later, Italy's 'Secolo' carried a report saying that two rivals, with motives of jealousy and the love of a woman Valentino had captivated, had laced his food with small quantities of poison—leaving, of course, no trace after it had been absorbed. Police in America, it was revealed, were carrying out secret investigations.

So secret, in fact, that no-one ever heard of them again.

THIRTY

Love wol nat ben constreyned by maistrye;
Whan maistrie comth, the god of love anon
Beteth hise winges, and farewell! he is gon!
Geoffrey Chaucer (1340–1400)

HAVING SENT AHEAD the biggest floral tribute of all—a
massive and massively-expensive concoction of red roses
with her name picked out in white—Pola Negri descended on New York to say a personal farewell to her
beloved Rudy. It was a sensational performance.

When her train drew into Grand Central Station on
the day before the funeral, she emerged in mourning
weeds of stunning severity which, a handy Press agent
revealed, had cost 3,000 dollars. Weeping, and supported
by a maid and Mrs. George Ullman, she walked slowly to
the barrier where she screamed and promptly fell into a
faint. Half-carried to a waiting car, she was driven to the
Ambassador Hotel, where Rudy had been so cruelly
stricken down, and promptly fell into another faint.

Recovered, she left for the funeral parlour and
through the still-waiting crowds into the Gold Room,
where her love lay waiting. At the sight of him she had to
be physically supported by attendants, and after kneeling
in prayer, she moaned and wept and collapsed. But she
was soon well enough to tell reporters: 'My love for
Valentino was the greatest love of my life. I shall never
forget him. I loved him not as one artist loves another,

but as a woman loves a man.'

Then, in wretched condition, she was led away.

*   *   *

In nomine Patris, et Filii et Spiritus Sancti ...

The priest's words broke the silence in the actors' church of St. Malachy. 'In the Name of the Father, and of the Son, and of the Holy Ghost...' In front of him lay the rose-covered coffin of the man who had caused so much chaos and comment during the last few days and who now, like any other mere mortal, was to receive the last blessing and farewell of his holy mother church in the solemn sacrifice of the Mass.

Kyrie eleison, Christie eleison ...

'Lord have mercy, Christ have mercy...' Except that even this seemed to some like some star-studded show-business occasion mounted for a curious, morbid public. Thirty minutes earlier, crowds had watched as the silver and bronze coffin was carried from the funeral church and placed in the hearse. Then, with an escort of twelve motor-cycle police, it set off slowly through streets lined with people, pushing, clambering, manoeuvering to get a better vantage point for the last farewell.

In the car behind the hearse they spotted Pola Negri, a tragic figure in black, her face hidden in her handkerchief, being comforted by the Ullmans. Behind her car came others with Jean Acker and Mary Pickford and Norma and Constance Talmadge and Nora Van Horn, representing Natacha Rambova.

All along the two-mile route police struggled to keep back spectators who gathered to watch the passing show, and the area around the church on West Forty-Ninth Street had been closed to all other traffic. That was where you spotted the most celebrities as they arrived to take their tickets-only pews: Douglas Fairbanks, George Jessel, Gloria Swanson, Bonnie Glass, Marilyn Miller ... some five hundred of them, and many of them faces you knew like your own.

Requiem aeternam dona eis, Domine, et lux perpetua luceat eis ...

'Eternal rest grant unto them, O Lord, and let perpetual light shine upon them.'

In between the priest's solemn intonations, you could hear the sobs and sniffles, the scratching of pens as reporters noted down the details of dresses and outfits and behaviour in grief: Pola Negri, who had to be helped up the aisle to her place, looked at times as though she might collapse. Jean Acker did faint, and had to be assisted to the door. A white-coated doctor and nurse stood by in case of emergency caused by emotion.

Ite Missa est ... 'Go, the Mass is ended!' The injunction came as a relief and the congregation muttered their reply.

'Deo gratias.'

The coffin was taken once more back to the funeral church to await its last journey, and Pola Negri retired to her hotel to hide her sorrow in silence. But not for long. Soon, between sobs, she was reading to reporters a letter written by Dr. Meeker which had lately come into her possession:

Dear Miss Negri;

I am asking Mary Pickford, an old friend and patient of mine, to deliver this message to you ... About 4 o'clock Monday morning I was sitting by Rudolph alone in the room. He opened his eyes, put out his hand and said 'I'm afraid we won't go fishing together. Perhaps we will meet again—who knows?' This was the first and only time he realised he would not get well. He was perfectly clear in his mind. He gave me a message for the Chief, Mr. Schenck, and then said: 'Pola—if she doesn't come in time, tell her I think of her.' Then he spoke in Italian and went into his long sleep. I feel an obligation to get this message to you.

Yours sincerely,
Harold D. Meeker.

She said no more. Merely read the letter and withdrew. But the meaning she intended to convey was quite clear to those who heard it: she was Rudy's last love.

And who else should be waiting on the dock on September 1 to greet Valentino's brother Alberto as he arrived to see him buried? Pola Negri, dressed in black, kissed and embraced him before, with tears in her eyes, she went with him to the funeral church to see the body. Afterwards, with the heartfelt thanks of those who feared that he would be taken away from them and buried in some far-flung Italian town with a strange name, Alberto announced: 'My brother belonged to America and his resting place will be in California, which he loved. My sister feels this way, too.'

And so, next day, Rudolph Valentino set off on his last journey by train to his final resting place, accompanied by Alberto, Pola and the Ullmans. All along the route, people looked out for the train, hoping to see something of the coffin, and when it arrived in Chicago, thousands turned up at the station to pay their respects.

In the Church of the Good Shepherd in Beverly Hills, on the morning of September 7, an opera star sang *Ave Maria* at the Mass before burial. Thousands lined the route from the church to the Hollywood Cemetery, where June Mathis had said Valentino could be buried in her family crypt until a permanent resting place could be decided upon.

A plane buzzed overhead dropping blossoms to the ground as Alberto said a silent prayer and Pola wept. The cameras whirred. Celebrities sobbed. A priest spoke the final words. The coffin was moved into the crypt and the marble slab lifted into place. 'You can rest here, Rudy, until I die,' June Mathis whispered. The world had seen, but not heard, the last of Rudolph Valentino.

THIRTY-ONE

Parting is all we know of heaven
And all we need of hell

Emily Dickinson (1830–86)

RUDY MIGHT BE dead but, according to one allegedly re-
liable source, he was certainly not taking it lying down.
In fact, declared American psychic Dr. George Benjamin
Wehner, he was having the time of his life (or death) in
the Great Blue Yonder and making frequent excursions
to mingle with lesser, living, mortals on Earth.

The revelations came, apparently, via Dr. Wehner in
spirit messages from the late lamented star himself and
featured prominently in *Rudy*, the intimate memoirs of
Natacha, first published in London—and later America
—soon after his death.

And although there were, of course, cynics who said
the messages were total tosh, and even that Natacha, in
death as in life, was putting words into Valentino's
mouth, a curious public was intrigued enough to pay out
ten shillings and sixpence to read how he was 'living' beyond the grave—and how much he preferred to stay
There, than to visit Here:

'Once,' he revealed of a journey to this world, 'I jolted
into a woman who had headed straight into me, and she
shuddered and grasped her companion's arm, saying
"My, what a cold wind struck me!" ' This made me furious. So death had turned me into a cold wind! I would

233

not have it so. I rushed up to a group of actors standing on the corner of Forty-Seventh Street and Broadway, near the Palace Theatre. I seized one of the men by the arm and shouted "I am Rudolph Valentino!" But he paid no attention and went on laughing and talking.'

He got no more satisfaction, it seemed, when he dropped in to see his movies. 'I sometimes find myself in theatres where my pictures are still being shown. But somehow they do not seem as real to me as they used to. I do not feel so stirred when an audience is moved by my acting, or the acting of others.'

Even so, he could understand now why the public were so fascinated by him. 'It turns out that the unusual magnetism I possessed when appearing on the screen was due to the fact that I have been an actor in previous lives.'

And Up There was an actor's paradise. 'My friends have taken me to see the theatres. They are enormous and very, very beautiful. They are built of thought substance, but of that thought substance which comes from true poets' ideals. All the great actors act in them. But there is a strange difference in the acting of here and the acting of earth.

'On the earth plane,' Rudy told his ghost-writer, 'a clever actor can portray any part given him by the manager. Not so here. There is no mere cleverness here. All is sincerity ... a man cannot play a king unless he is majestic in character and soul. On earth, the Passion Play comes nearest to this sincere expression.'

Up There, all was lovely. 'So much love I have never seen before. Everyone seems to beam with it. Caruso, whom, as you remember, I always admired so, comes to see me frequently. I am not sure whether he comes to me or I go to him. When I asked him about it, he laughed and said "Well, *mio figlio*, what does it matter? Are we not together?" He does not look just as he used to, either. He looks more like his music sounded, if you can imagine what I mean.'

What Valentino infuriatingly did not reveal, however, was if he and Enrico ever got together to sing the songs written about them after their demise: 'They Needed a Songbird in Heaven, so God took Caruso Away' and, for Rudy, 'There's a New Star in Heaven Tonight'.

It would have made an angelic musical occasion.

Meanwhile, back down on Earth, all was not peace and light. They were going through Valentino's affairs and finding them a mess of debt. To his credit were two houses and land, valued at 240,000 dollars, four large cars (40,000 dollars) and four small ones (unvalued), eight horses (4,000 dollars), 12 dogs (10,000 dollars), a yacht (6,000 dollars), jewellery (40,000 dollars), costumes and furniture (12,000 dollars), an insurance policy (40,000 dollars) and an estimated 1,400,000 dollars from films. Unvalued were his collection of firearms and birds from two aviaries, 1,000 pairs of socks, 300 ties and cravats, 40 suits, 50 pairs of shoes, 20 hats, three fur coats, seven watches and several hundred shirts.

George Ullman moved in to make the debt a profit. In big auctions, he sold off Valentino 'junk' worth around 28,000 dollars for some 76,000 dollars. An adoring public, who had now elevated their idol from the Great Lover to the God of Love, with shrines to his memory in their homes, clamoured to have a relic of the true Rudy ... a sock, a handkerchief, a tie, a garter. His paperback books—with a newly-printed 'Rudolph Valentino' book-plate freshly inserted on Ullman's orders—went for five dollars, ten dollars and even more. 'When Valentino died,' Ullman's lawyer reported, 'he owed the Art Cinema 132,000 dollars. His estate was covered with liens, mortgages and everything else. The only thing he really did own was all but two shares in his producing company. Ullman was secretary and treasurer, and the only thing the corporation owned were two pictures. Out of these Ullman has made about 400,000 dollars for the estate, by showing them everywhere—even in China, where they don't know that Rudolph is dead.'

George Ullman, who would go through years of mounting work and legal fights in clearing up the estate of the man he helped to success, died in September, 1975. His son Daniel, a favourite of Valentino, still lives in Los Angeles.

Alberto and Maria had a third share in the will with Mrs. Werner, whom Valentino wanted to thank for her kindness after Natacha left to get her divorce. Maria married an Italian architect and Alberto, changing his name to Albert Valentino and his nose by plastic surgery in operations similar to one previously performed on Jack Dempsey, went into movies. He did it, he said, on the advice of June Mathis. But his one film was far from good and soon forgotten.

Jean Acker was not mentioned in the will. 'I didn't expect to be,' she told reporters who so recently had believed that she might again become Valentino's wife.

Natacha Rambova fared little better. She received the sum of one dollar—'this sum and no more,' as Valentino decreed in his will—and showed neither anger nor surprise. 'Rudy,' she said, 'has explained everything. I understand.' But she had a lot more to say, in her book, about accusations that she had sacrificed Valentino's career for her own selfish ambitions to become a power in the film world.

Her fault, she claimed, was not ambition but conceit. 'I was conceited enough to imagine that I could force the producers into giving Rudy the kind of production which our artistic ambitions called for. I could not understand why, with his ability, romance, magnetism and proved drawing power, Rudy should not have the best—why he should continually be thrust into small, trifling, cheap, commercial pictures, while other artists of much less ability and popularity were given big stories and big productions. The injustice of it made me furious, and I stubbornly made up my mind that he should not be used so.'

In 1934, Natacha married a Spanish nobleman, Don Alvaro de Urzaiz. They were later divorced and she went back to America to live with her widowed mother. Selling up the villa in France, she said she could no longer bear its associations with Valentino and the constant stream of fashionably-dressed women who arrived there from all over the world, bringing flowers and begging to be allowed to inspect the house, to touch his clothes, to sit on his favourite chairs.

Natacha died in hospital at Pasadena, California, at the age of 69, in June, 1966. She rated a sixteen-line obituary in *The Times*. But they managed to spell her name wrong.

June Mathis was at a theatre in New York in July, 1927, when she collapsed and died. The tragedy brought a problem about Valentino's resting place, for she had said he could lie in her crypt 'until I die'. It was solved when his body was moved to an adjoining crypt, reserved for Miss Mathis's husband, Sylvano Balboni, but which was eventually bought by the Guglielmi family. Even then there was little peace: women made their way to the grave from all parts of America and the world—one

237

wife living in mid-America sued for divorce on the grounds that her husband would not let her live near the mausoleum. Vandals chipped pieces from the vault, a marble pedestal was broken and its chips sold as Valentino souvenirs, and five men discovered trying to break into the crypt were suspected to be 'ghouls, planning to steal the body of Valentino for commercial purposes'.

A memorial to Valentino—a symbolic bronze nude, standing on a globe and with its head gazing towards the sky—also became the target for vandals after its unveiling in Hollywood's De Longpre Park in May 1930. After being toppled twice from its plinth, it was removed by park staff for safe-keeping.

The Lady in Black, who was to mystify Pressmen for years, first appeared when she knelt in prayer before the statue on an early anniversary of Valentino's death. One of several mourners clad entirely in black, and carrying red roses, she paid her tribute at the crypt every year. But it was not until November 1945 that she was revealed as Marion Wilson—the former Ziegfeld Follies beauty Marion Benda, who said she had been with Valentino at the Warburton party before he was taken ill. Now Marion herself was ill in a Hollywood hospital after taking an overdose of sleeping tablets, and a cousin revealed much more than the fact that she was 'the lady in black'.

Marion, he said, was married to Valentino a year before he died, but it was kept secret 'for fear it would hurt his romantic appeal'. They had a daughter born in Europe who was living in London, the cousin claimed. For years, Marion had tried to get her daughter to live in America and, depressed when she failed to do so, had been taking drugs to help her sleep. Now, delirious, she was calling her name over again and again.

The daughter never appeared, and Marion vanished from the headlines until the 1951 anniversary, when she fainted at the tomb. Then, in the December of that year, she was found dead at her Hollywood apartment. A relative said: 'She had talked more and more of Valentino lately. Over and over again, I heard her say softly to herself: "He always said I was too beautiful to live."' Her story about being married to the star? Untrue, he said.

Carmel Meyers, already a star when Valentino was struggling for recognition, is still a much sought-after actress and television personality. In the beautifully-furnished apartment between Hollywood and the Pacific coast, where she lives alone, she says: 'It's hard to believe so many years have passed since Rudy was alive. I thought he was wonderful. He had such personality and style. And that voice of his sent shivers running right through me. My only regret is that I was too young to be allowed to socialise with him. It was a tragedy that he died so young, just when he was reaching his peak as an actor. But Rudy was one of those people who will always be remembered by those who knew him. You couldn't exaggerate either his talent or his personality. He was one of the truly great ones.'

Viola Dana retired many years ago and left the Beverly Hills house she shared with her sister during Valentino's lifetime. Now, in her luxurious home at Santa Monica, ten miles from the Hollywood studios where she was a star in the Twenties, she remembers: 'They called Rudy the Great Lover. I would call him the Great Dancer. He was supreme on the dance floor. He was such a splendid person, and all man. But no-one could understand his first marriage. Perhaps he didn't understand too well himself. It was sad to see him unhappy, because he wasn't the kind of person anyone likes to see

239

suffer. He was one of the lovely vibrant people who kept us all amused. But nobody ever knew very much about Valentino. He was too much of a loner. Anyone who says different is lying.'

Gertrude Astor, also long retired from the screen, lives the life of a semi-recluse in Hollywood, preferring people to remember her as she was. Reluctant to meet strangers, she could not bring herself to appear for an interview, but agreed to talk on the telephone. 'As far as I was concerned,' she said, 'Rudy was very all right. He was very conceited inside, but didn't show it. He knew what his future was and he took good care of himself. Except for his marriages. His first marriage was difficult to figure out, but the second was even less comprehensible. That was ridiculous. He was making the same mistake all over again. It was all very hard to understand, because he really knew what to do with a woman. His reputation wasn't just founded on playacting, believe me!'

Pola Negri lives with her memories in San Antonio, Texas, rarely granting interviews, seldom talking of Valentino. But she remembers him as 'a wonderful human being—a man. Off-screen he was quiet, even reserved. But he was charming. He had tremendous sex-appeal, and an uncanny fascination for audiences. There is no-one who can touch him today as a screen hero or lover. There is no-one like Valentino.'

Castellaneta, where the terrible beauty was born, is changed, changed utterly. Where once there were narrow, dusty tracks, there are clean, well-kept roads and the Bari–Taranto motorway is just three minutes away. While Rome was once apparently at the other end of the earth, you can reach it now, by road and plane, within three hours. Where once there were few places for young people to spend their leisure hours, except two or three little cafés, or the beach seven miles away, to which they would hitch-hike by cart, or horse or donkey, there are now cinemas and all the other entertainment facilities of modern life, and the once barely-attended beach is a lure for thousands of holidaymakers.

'Castellaneta,' says municipal official Mario Gravini, proudly surveying the town today, 'was once poor, even bleak. Towns like ours were forbidding, with an air of being forgotten. There was nothing for young people to do. The place was in a stagnant state. Today, the building boom is great. We have light industry, metal-mechanics. The olive-groves are well-tended and productive, like the orange-groves near the sea. We have developed our own vineyards, and produce a modest red wine— "vino primitivo". In those days perhaps only a couple of local constables strolled about. Now we have fully-manned posts of the national and ordinary police. But there is little crime, no violence. Youth is well-behaved.'

Few unsolved mysteries bother the mind of Marshal-Major Giovanni Cardenio, Commander of the Caribinieri national police in Castellaneta. But, in his office, he talks of one that still intrigues him: 'A great mass of beautiful flowers used to arrive here every year on the anniversary of Valentino's death,' he says. 'They came from the time he died, every year without fail, and were placed on the family tomb. We knew they came from London, and were despatched through Interflora to Taranto and brought here by van. But who sent them was a mystery. We once tried to discover the identity of the mystery woman—it must have been a woman, surely? We never succeeded. Then, in 1972, the flowers did not arrive. Nor have they come since. We assumed that the loyal admirer had died. We were very sad ...'

241

There is little in Castellaneta to remind people that it was the birthplace of one of the screen's most historic personalities. It was not until 1956 that the town publicly accepted the fact—and only then after a political row involving Mayor Gabriele Semeraro, now sixty-three, a Christian Democrat MP in the House of Deputies and the leading citizen of Castellaneta for thirty-eight years. He campaigned for a great bronze statue of Valentino to honour the town's most famous son. The opposition was totally against spending money on an actor. Saints and statesmen, yes. A film star, never. Besides, they argued, there was bitterness among some people, who said that Valentino, unlike most other emigrants, had not sent a penny back home, even at the height of his success. So why should the town pay money to honour him now?

In the end, though, the mayor won the day and had his way: a ceramic statue of the star, produced by Rome sculptor Luigi Gheno, was unveiled on a park terrace overlooking the countryside, with a series of murals depicting the motion-picture world in which he found fame. It is a few yards from the street named after him, the Via Rodolpho Valentino—there is also a Cinema Valentino and a Bar Rudy—and not far away is the house in which he was born. Via Roma 116 is now the home of Vito Staffieri and his wife Lippolis, and their two young children. But they are seldom disturbed by sightseers. Visitors to Castellaneta call, mostly in the summertime, for not more than half-an-hour, look at the plaque on the wall outside the front door which announces 'The actor Rudolph Valentino was born here,' stroll around the little park and leave. There is little to detain them.

Rita Maldarizzi is glad they don't call on her and Ada. The sisters, now seventy and sixty-six, prefer to be alone with their memories of him. 'Thank God the tourists don't bother us,' Rita says at her home in the Via Ospedale, 'even though we are the only people still living who had such close contact with him in his early days. He was in our home more often than he was in his own. He was always hanging around. My father said he didn't have the slightest intention of doing work of any kind. He didn't go out and look for it, certainly—just sat around all day with other boys at the cafés. But he did have this obsession to go to America. He had heard so many tales of success, fortunes being made, and dollars. Everything was dollars to him, and if he'd lived today he would have been off to Hollywood all the faster.

'I think he got all his wild ideas from his mother, Donna Beatrice. When she was carrying him, right up to almost the last month of her pregnancy, she'd be dancing. She was a wild, happy, beautiful woman, always cheerful, laughing, dancing. That's what gave Rudolpho this funny head of his, always wanting to do wild things, running off and making dollars. Everyone said the same in those days: "It's because his mother was always dancing."

'I'll never forget the day he brought that woman back to town. He must have been in his teens then, perhaps sixteen or seventeen. He brought this girl here. She was a pretty young thing, one of those roving folk singers, and he escorted her round the streets all day. What a sensation he was. It was sheer impudence. But we knew he'd never marry a local girl and settle down. His main fascination was always the tales of emigrants, the good life overseas, making fortunes, earning stacks and stacks of dollars. He simply made that dream come true.

'That day he came back, after he'd become famous, we girls were thrilled by his lofty talk, dizzy listening to his stories of Hollywood. There was no cinema here in those

243

days and we had never seen a film. What he spoke of seemed to be a fairytale world to us. But he had changed. He was wholly different. Everything about him seemed so strange, so theatrical. We cried when he had gone. A short time later our father died, and we had a long message of condolence from Rudolph, but we never heard from him again. We knew, somehow, that we never would.

'But we still have the coffee service that Mama brought out when he came, and the divan on which he lay back, telling those stories. Of course, we've since seen an old film or two of his recently, screened as a curiosity. We could see that it was him on the screen, naturally. But it wasn't our real Rodolpho. He'd changed so much from the time he was a boy in Castellaneta...'

APPENDIX: RUDOLPH VALENTINO'S FILMS

Alimony (1st Nat'l 1918). Directed by Emmett J. Flynn. With Josephine Whittel, Lois Wilson, George Fisher, Ida Lewis. Valentino's first screen appearance was as an extra; he was merely atmospheric ballroom background.

A Society Sensation (Universal 1918). Directed by Paul Powell. With Carmel Myers, Alfred Allen, Fred Kelsey, Harold Goodwin, Zazu Pitts. Valentino was billed as M. Rudolphe de Valentina.

All Night (Universal 1918). Directed by Paul Powell. With Carmel Myers, Charles Dorian, Mary Warren, William Dyer, Wadsworth Harris, Jack Hall.

The Delicious Little Devil (Universal 1919). Directed by Robert Z. Leonard. With Mae Murray, Harry Rattenbury, Richard Cummings, Ivor McFadden, Bertram Gassby. Mae Murray got him the part.

A Rogue's Romance (Vitagraph 1919). Directed by James Young. With Earle Williams, Brinsley Shaw, Herbert Standing, Katherine Adams, Maude George. From an H. H. Van Loan story.

The Homebreaker (Ince–Paramount 1919). Directed by Victor Schertzinger. With Dorothy Dalton, Douglas Maclean, Edwin Stevens. Most of Valentino's role ended on the cutting-room floor.

Virtuous Sinners (Pioneer 1919). Directed by Emmett J. Flynn. With Norman Kerry, Wanda Hawley, Harry Holden, Bert Woodruff. Valentino is only to be glimpsed as background, although Flynn kept him on the payroll throughout shooting.

The Big Little Person (Universal 1919). Directed by Robert Z. Leonard. With Mae Murray.

Out of Luck (Griffith–Artcraft 1919). Directed by Elmer

Clifton. With Dorothy Gish, Ralph Graves, Raymond Canon, George Fawcett, Emily Chichester, Porter Strong, Kate V. Toncray.

Eyes of Youth (Equity 1919). Directed by Albert Parker. With Clara Kimball Young, Milton Sills, Edmund Lowe, Gareth Hughes, Pauline Starke, Sam Southern, Ralph Lewis. Based upon the Max Marcin–Charles Guernon play which had starred Marjorie Rambeau on Broadway.

The Married Virgin (Fidelity 1920). Directed by Joseph Maxwell. With Vera Sisson, Edward Jobson, Frank Newburg, Kathleen Kirkham, Lillian Leighton. Actually Valentino's second film, but release was held up by litigation. Reissued 1922 as 'Frivolous Wives'.

An Adventuress (Rep. Dist Co. 1920). Directed by Fred J. Balshofer. With Julian Eltinge, Virginia Rappe, Leo White. Reissued 1922 as 'The Isle of Love'.

The Cheater (MGM 1920). Directed by Henry Otto. With May Allison, King Baggott, Frank Currier, Harry Van Meter. An adaptation of Henry Arthur Jones' play 'Judah'.

Passion's Playground (1st Nat'l 1920). Directed by J. A. Barry. With Katherine MacDonald, Norman Kerry, Nell Craig, Edwin Stevens, Alice Wilson, Virginia Ainsworth, Howard Gaye. Adapted from a C. N. and M. A. Williamson novel.

Once to Every Woman (Universal 1920). Directed by Allan J. Holubar. With Dorothy Phillips, Wr. Ellingford, Margaret Mann, Emily Chichester, Elinor Field, Robert Anderson.

Stolen Moments (Pioneer 1920). Directed by James Vincent. With Marguerite Namara.

The Wonderful Chance (Selznick 1920). Directed by George Archainbaud. With Eugene O'Brien, Martha Mansfield, Tom Blake, Joe Flanagian, Warren Cook. Adapted from an H. H. Van Loan story.

The Four Horsemen of the Apocalypse (MGM 1920). Directed by Rex Ingram. With Alice Terry, Joseph Swickhard, John Sainpolis, Alan Hale, Wallace Beery, Stuart Holmes, Jean Hersholt, Mabel Van Buren, Nigel de Brulier. Valentino's first starring role, that of Julio Desnoyers. A June Mathis adaptation of the Ibanez novel.

Uncharted Seas (MGM 1921). Directed by Wesley Ruggles.

With Alice Lake, Carl Gerard, Fred Turner, Charles Mailes, Rhea Haines.

Camille (MGM 1921). Directed by Ray C. Smallwood. With Nazimova, Arthur Hoyt, Zeffie Tillbury, Rex Cherryman, Edward Connelly, (Patsy) Ruth Miller, William Orland, Consuelo Flowerton, Mrs. Oliver. Valentino played Armand in this June Mathis modern version of the Dumas *fils* novel and play, with settings designed by Natacha Rambova.

The Conquering Power (MGM 1921). Directed by Rex Ingram. With Alice Terry, Ralph Lewis, Eric Mayne, Edna Demaury. A June Mathis adaptation of Balzac's 'Eugenie Grandet'.

The Sheik (Paramount 1921). Directed by George Melford. With Agnes Ayres, Adolph Menjou, Walter Long, Lucien Littlefield, George Wagner, (Patsy) Ruth Miller, R. R. Butler. Adapted from E. M. Hull's popular novel.

Moran of the Lady Letty (Paramount 1922). Directed by George Melford. With Dorothy Dalton, Walter Long, Charles Brindley, Maude Wayne. An adaptation of the Frank Norris novel.

Beyond the Rocks (Paramount 1922). Directed by Sam Wood. With Gloria Swanson, Alec B. Francis, Edythe Chapman, Gertrude Astor, Mabel Van Buren, Helen Dunbar, June Elvidge. Written by Elinor Glyn.

Blood and Sand (Paramount 1922). Directed by Fred Niblo. With Lila Lee, Nita Naldi, Walter Long, Charles Belcher, George Feld, Rose Rosanova, Leo White. A June Mathis adaptation of the Ibanez novel.

The Young Rajah (Paramount 1922). Directed by Philip Rosen. With Wanda Hawley, Pat Moore, Charles Ogle, Fanny Midgely, Robert Ober, Joseph Swickard, Bertram Grassby, J. Farrell MacDonald, George Periolat, George Field, Maude Wayne, William Boyd, Spottiswoode Aitken.

Monsieur Beaucaire (Paramount 1924). Directed by Sidney Olcott. With Bebe Daniels, Doris Kenyon, Lois Wilson, Lowell Sherman, Paulette du Val, Flora Finch. Adapted from Booth Tarkington's novelette.

A Sainted Devil (Paramount 1924). Directed by Joseph Henaberry. With Nita Naldi, Helena d'Algy, Dagmar Godowsky, Jean del Val, George Seigmann, Louise Lagrange. Adapted from Rex Beach's 'Rope's End'.

Cobra (Paramount–Ritz–Carlton 1925). Directed by Joseph Henaberry. With Nita Naldi, Casson Ferguson, Gertrude Olmstead, Hector V. Sarno, Claire de Lorez, Eileen Percy, Lillian Langdon, Henry Barrows, Rose Rosanova.

The Eagle (U-A 1925). Directed by Clarence Brown. With Vilma Banky, Louise Dresser, Albert Conti, James Marcus, George Nichols, Carrie Clark Ward. Adapted from Pushkin's 'Dubrovsky' by Hans Kraly.

Son of the Sheik (U-A 1926). Directed by George Fitzmaurice. With Vilma Banky, Agnes Ayres, George Fawcett, Montagu Love, Karl Dane, Bull Montana. Adapted by Frances Marion from E. M. Hull's sequel to her successful earlier novel.

SUNSHINE

Norma Klein 50p

Jacquelyn Helton died in 1971 of a rare from of cancer. She was 20 years old. During the last 18 months of her life she kept a diary as a legacy for her baby daughter.

Inspired by the story of her courage, Universal Studios produced a stunning television film based closely on her diary. The day after it was shown, a whole nation was talking about it. 'It literally bursts with the joy and fulfilment of living,' said the Los Angeles Times; and the Buffalo Evening News called it 'Something very special.'

Norma Klein's novel has been written from the actual diary and Carol Sobieski's script for the film. The story has since become a cinema film which broke box-office records; and it is the inspiration of a new television series.

The enormous impact of Sunshine is easy to understand. it is a simple, true story which has touched the hearts of millions of people the world over.

Use the special order form at the end of this book

Re-live the memories of Meg's motel

CROSSROADS – A NEW BEGINNING

Malcolm Hulke 40p

'I NAME THIS MOTEL CROSSROADS, AND GOD BLESS ALL WHO STAY HERE!'

So began the television phenomenon of the sixties and seventies. More than seven million homes tune in every time Crossroads is broadcast.

Malcolm Hulke is another success story. A member of the Crossroads scriptwriting team, and script editor of the serial for four years, he is also the author of several bestselling books.

Now he has created a heartwarming series of novels based on the Crossroads scripts.

For long-standing fans the books bring back a flood of memories; and for recent converts they fill in the background to Meg's motel. They also tell the stories the programme glossed over; and show the scenes television could not screen.

Also available

CROSSROADS – A WARM BREEZE 45p
CROSSROADS – A TIME FOR LOVING 50p
CROSSROADS – SOMETHING OLD,
                            SOMETHING NEW 50p

Use the special order form at the end of this book

Rock on with Everest

SO YOU WANT TO BE IN THE MUSIC BUSINESS

Tony Hatch 90p

ARE YOU the next superstar? Is your son? Your grand-daughter? Your neighbour?

Fame and fortune are waiting for someone who is now stuck in a dead-end job dreaming of stardust.

Have *you* got what it takes? And if you have, do you know what to do about it?

Tony Hatch does.

He started as a tea-boy in a music publisher's office. Today he is right at the top: a highly-paid composer, arranger and record-producer with a string of hits under his belt.

Lately he has become even more famous for his perceptive straight-talking on TV's talent show New Faces.

Now he has put everything he learned from 15 successful years in showbusiness into one entertaining, revealing book.

Use the special order form at the end of this book

So you want to be a DJ?

THE DJ HANDBOOK

Emperor Rosko 95p

You want to play records for the millions — talk to people every day in their homes — become a face the public instantly recognise — enjoy the glamour and rewards of stardom.

But where do you start? What equipment do you need? How do you get your first DJ job?

Emperor Rosko begins by telling how *he* made it to the top of this supercharged profession.

Then he shows how *you* can travel the same road:

HOW TO promote yourself;

WHERE TO get free records;

WHO TO write to at the BBC;

HOW TO cope with the technical side of DJ-ing.

The Head of Radio One, Derek Chinnery, says: 'This is the most comprehensive book of its kind ever written.'

It is *the* how-to-do-it book for disc jockeys — by the most successful DJ in Europe.

Use the special order form at the end of this book

From the master frightener himself

**THE BORIS KARLOFF
HORROR
ANTHOLOGY**   50p

WHAT IS the essence of a good horror story?
'The ability of story and author to entrance one's
conscious from the here and now, the mundane, into
those other worlds of fear, terror and black magic.'
So says Boris Karloff in his introduction to this chilling
collection.

*And this is the yardstick he has used to choose the
twelve most dreadful stories ever written.*

Here is Edgar Allan Poe, with a tale of ghastly revenge
in a crypt; August Derleth, with a nebulous monster
from prehistory; Theodore Sturgeon and a strange
encounter in a cemetery; C. M. Kornbluth's little boy
with a worm in his mind; Robert Silverberg's story of a
living man buried in a coffin; Robert Bloch's holy
statue with terrible powers; H. P. Lovecraft's Haunter
of the Dark; and more.

As soon as the book is in your hands you can say, like
Boris Karloff: 'I look forward to being scared out of
my wits.'

Use the special order form at the end of this book

Death by nightmare

THE SLEEPWALK KILLERS

Leslie Watkins   50p

Simon Fraser, a Scottish millworker, was a quiet and
gentle man who adored his baby son. One night he
got up at 3 a.m. and battered the 18-month-old child
to death.

A jury found him Not Guilty of murder – because he
had been asleep at the time.

Millions of people walk in their sleep. Their behaviour
becomes a family joke. But for a handful of them, the
joke turns to horror.

Sleepwalking violence has occurred from Aberdeen to
Arkansas. The sufferers have often been cleared of
murder. Daily Mail journalist Leslie Watkins has taken a
special interest in this ever since he covered the
killing of a young girl in Essex by a sleeping American
airman.

Watkins has interviewed the relatives of sleepwalk
killers, dug up yellowing court records, and searched
newspaper files all over the world. The result is a
definitive book on a little-known but terrifying
phenomenon.

Use the special order form at the end of this book

The funniest movie for years!

KEEP IT UP DOWNSTAIRS

Elton Hawke 60p

UPSTAIRS the elderly Lord Cockshute — drunk, broke and trouserless — is chasing Mimi the maid, who has somehow lost her uniform.

DOWNSTAIRS gamekeeper Mellons and the parlourmaid have found an interesting new way to make daisy chains.

UPSTAIRS Lady Kitty is avoiding the clutches of the revolting Snotty Shuttlecock, to whom the family owe money.

DOWNSTAIRS the groom also has designs upon Kitty, and he is strangely jealous of a black stallion called Ramrod.

UPSTAIRS the wealthy American Durenecks come and stay, and stay and come . . .

DOWNSTAIRS Hampton, the faithful butler, is desperately trying to conceal the truth about his sinful past.

UPSTAIRS Viscount Standfast is experimenting with rubber in his laboratory; but he can't think of an application for his latest unusual invention . . .

ILLUSTRATED with pages of hilarious photographs from the film starring Diana Dors and William Rushton.

Use the special order form at the end of this book

Armchair bookshop

All good bookshops stock Everest titles. If you have any difficulty getting our books – or if you prefer to shop from home – please fill in this form.

———————

To: Armchair bookshop, Everest Books, 4 Valentine Place, London SE1.

Please send me the following titles. I enclose purchase price plus 15p (postage & packing) by cheque, postal or money order (no currency).

....

....

....

....

....

....

....

———————

NAME (*block letters*) ....

ADDRESS ....

....

....

....

———————